# First Citizen Smyth

## NOEL I. DAVIDSON

**AMBASSADÓR**
**Belfast • Greenville**

First Citizen Smyth
Copyright © 1996 Noel Davidson

First published 1996

ISBN  1  898787  63  8

**AMBASSADOR PRODUCTIONS LTD.**
Providence House
16 Hillview Avenue,
Belfast, BT5 6JR
United Kingdom

Emerald House
1 Chick Springs Road, Suite 102
Greenville, South Carolina 29609
United States of America

OTHER BOOKS BY THE AUTHOR
My Father's Hand
This Is For Real
Just The Way I Am
Some Party in Heaven

# INTRODUCTION

*"If you can talk with the crowds and keep your virtue,*
*Or walk with kings - nor lose the common touch,*
*If neither foes nor loving friends can hurt you,*
*If all men count with you, but none too much."*

These lines from Britain's most popular poem, "If", by Rudyard Kipling, aptly describe Councillor Rev. Eric Smyth, Lord Mayor of Belfast, 1995-1996.

When I first met him, he was close to tears.

It was Thursday 14th September, 1995.

As he talked frankly of all the events of that day I knew I was going to like this man. His simple Christian sincerity was so obvious.

"Brother," he began. ("Brother!" and I had only ever been talking to him for an hour).

"Brother, how can I go on? They are all out to get me ..."

It so happened that on that very afternoon his son Keith had been sentenced to nine months imprisonment for drugs offences. An older son Mark, was already "inside".

"They," whom he felt were, "all out to get him" were the media, the devil, his political opponents.

He was depressed.

He was down. But not out.

"I'm sure God has some purpose in all of this," he admitted, perhaps somewhat reluctantly.

We prayed together.

It was a bonding experience.

Since that memorable first night, we have met often, and shared much.

I have heard about many of the people in the Lord Mayor's life.

There are Frances, his wife, and six children ...

Donika and Matthew with their disabilities.

Royalty, a President and his wife, Lord Mayors of other cities, church and political leaders. The devoted Christian friends at the Jesus Saves Mission, and the ordinary, decent, hardworking people of the city.

I have met, and been helped by, his attentive staff at the City Hall. These are the people whom Eric once described to me as, "The ones who keep me right"!

The Lord Mayor has shared with me, too, as he did so candidly on our initial encounter, the problems in his life. He has told me often, "I want it all to go in, Noel. Hide nothing."

And I haven't.

There have been emotional problems with fostering and adoption, the problems of coping with disability, his own dyslexia and his children's handicaps, and of course, his sons and the drugs.

We have talked through the spiritual problems of a stuttering faith, a fear to witness, opposition from without and misgivings from within. The problems of helping to establish and maintain a church testimony.

The most striking thing about this genuine man, though, is the peace which pervades his life, no matter how busy that life seems to become.

This, he freely admits, comes from a daily, often hourly, contact with his God.

Eric Smyth became a Christian when a teenager, and the reality of his faith sustains him in his day-to-day work and witness.

This book, then, is the story of a most unlikely-looking lump of clay, chosen by God, the Master Potter, to perform a function for Him.

That clay was moulded and shaped on the wheel of His love to make it into something useful, then fired and baked in the kiln of adversity to make it into something strong.

May God bless it to you.

*Noel I. Davidson*
*1996*

# CONTENTS

~ CHAPTER ONE ~

# THE HAPPIEST DAYS
# OF YOUR LIFE?

---

THE SCIENCE TEACHER DELIVERED THE TEST PAPER ON TO
THE DESK OF A TWELVE-YEAR-OLD PUPIL WITH A RESOUND-
ING THUMP.

"Smyth, you will never make anything of yourself. You will certainly never get anywhere in this life," he announced.

Feeling perhaps that some explanation for his outburst was required, he went on, "I have never tried to read such utter rubbish in my
life. You obviously haven't understood one single word of what I have
been talking about all year."

Eric Smyth had more than a mere dislike for school. He hated it.

From the very first morning when he had been coaxed, crying,
into Lisnasharragh Primary School, and had followed his mother straight
out of it again, still crying, young Eric detested every day he was there.

He was shouted at in class because he could not learn, and then
bullied in the playground because he was considered "odd".

He made every possible excuse to miss school. Any part of his
anatomy that had even the slightest twinge of pain brought an, "Oh
mummy, I'm not very well this morning" type plea from the reluctant
scholar.

When "mummy" didn't rise to the bait, and she usually didn't, Eric often just "mitched" anyhow.

Eric's difficulty was with words. He couldn't read them. Letters on a page never made any sense to him. And when he couldn't read, he couldn't spell. And when he couldn't spell he couldn't write. Things were only set to get worse.

The science teacher had been partly right, partly wrong. He was dead right about what his pupil had written down. It was aptly described, "utter rubbish". Where he was wrong was when he stated that Eric hadn't "understood one single word of what he had been talking about". He had understood at least some of it, but he couldn't write it down.

It was all so frustrating. The boy was dyslexic.

In the days when young Eric went to school, however, they didn't have such a high-sounding tongue-twisting description for his condition.

To the teachers he was educationally sub-normal. ESN for short.

His mates had another word for it again. They just called him "stupid".

When he moved from Lisnasharragh Primary to Lisnasharragh Secondary School there were two subjects in which he enjoyed some measure of success. This meant that he was only mostly, rather than absolutely, miserable in school.

The first was his art. Eric liked to draw and paint. His ability with the paint brush qualified him as a set painter for the school plays. This was great because he was excused lessons in totally incomprehensible subjects like English and History, just to paint the scenery for dramatic productions.

Participation in all manner of sports was his second lifeline.

Eric loved physical education and he hero-worshipped the PE master. He sometimes dreamed of being one some day, but often wondered if PE teachers had to be able to read and write.

Games afternoons were a particular delight. An oasis in the desert. Light relief in days of drudgery.

In summer it was cricket, in winter it was football.

It was no problem whatsoever for young Eric to stay until four-thirty or five o'clock on a summer afternoon to practise for the cricket team.

On autumn and winter afternoons Eric and a group of his friends used to dally their way home from football matches and practices. They were never in any hurry. For those who could read and write and were even mildly interested in things academic, arriving home meant tea and then homework.

No need to rush for that!

Muddy boots tied together with multi-knotted muddy laces were slung over their shoulders. Muddy, sometimes wet, and often sweaty school strips peeped out of ravelled duffle bags. Most of the boys looked rather dishevelled.

The late afternoon returning-from-football pupil looked entirely different from the semi-tidy early morning going-to-school variety.

There were two topics of conversation amongst the boys as they ambled along. There was a sometimes topic and a mostly topic.

The "sometimes" topic was girls. And girl friends.

The "mostly" topic was football. Football players, football supporters, football teams.

The discussion of football would occasionally include glimpses into each individual's dream for his future.

There was one lad who seemed to have mega-ideas about himself.

Eric and the lads used to laugh at him when he said, "No fellas. I can't come out for a kick about after tea. I want to go to bed early."

What kind of a "mammy's boy" was this?

When the guffaws had subsided the young aspirant would go on, "You are laughing now, but you had better watch out. One day you will be seeing me on the T.V."

The rest of the boys laughed even more incredulously. Fingers were pointed at, then turned beside, tousled heads.

He was an extremely good player, there was no doubt about that, but in the days when televised football was a rare occurrence his prediction sounded rather preposterous.

Years later, though, those who mocked were forced to remember chilly evenings on the darkening streets of East Belfast.

They DID see their one-time team-mate on the T.V.

The boyish prophecy had been fulfilled.

He had kept his word.

His name was George Best.

# CHAPTER TWO

# THE MORMONS AND
# THE MILKMAN

---

ERIC WAS IMPRESSED BY THE TALL STRANGERS WHO CAME UP AROUND THE DOWNSHIRE ESTATE WHERE HE LIVED. THEY HAD SWANKY SUITS AND SPOKE WITH A PLEASANT AMERICAN DRAWL.

Although he hated school, Eric sometimes found that the days dragged on a bit in the summer holidays. Especially since he was rising each morning at five o'clock to go out on a milk run to make a bit of pocket money.

So these friendly foreigners were a welcome diversion in the humdrum summer days.

They appealed to the young teenager for two reasons. The first was the peculiar game which they taught the semi-bored youngsters to play. In it the bowler had a wee hard ball that he flung for all he was fit at the batter who played swipe at it with a bat the shape of the beetle his mother used to pound the clothes with on washdays, only a bit longer. If the batter should manage perchance to hit the ball as it hurtled towards him, then he set off on a run around a number of bases, laid out in a diamond shape.

It was a fascinating game.

"Baseball" was what they called it.

Secondly, these plausible preachers appealed to Eric because of their message. They talked about a man called Joseph Smith. This lucky namesake of his had apparently had a vision in which he had seen God. And talked to him. Now there was something different! To see God!

Eric liked that.

He thought that here was a mightily privileged man.

A man who had seen God.

He had never heard of anybody like this in his life before.

Maybe if he tagged along with these guys he would have some sort of fantastic revelation as well.

When the Mormon missionaries, as they described themselves, saw that the lad was interested in them, and what they had to say, they returned the compliment. By showing a particular interest in him.

In a few months, as a boy of thirteen, Eric was baptised into the Mormon faith, in a house in the Mount area of East Belfast.

As a Mormon convert he was now compelled to live by their creed. Obey the rules. He wasn't allowed to stray from the basic teaching of the Mormon church.

His new religious affiliation required that he observe a high moral code, coupled with some more down-to-earth demands.

The drinking of tea or coffee was not permitted. Caffeine was considered bad. Hence it was banned. Alcohol was totally taboo.

Adherence to this strict code of rules made young Eric feel that he was really doing something worthwhile.

So taken was this new convert initially that he started to promote Mormonism. He held "meetings" in the back garden with his pals.

The chap who could neither read or write was distributing leaflets to his friends with the exhortation,"This is powerful good, boy. You ought to read it!"

His original enthusiasm began to wane, however.

The discussion in the Religious Education class in school was the start of it. Religious Education had never been Eric's "pet" subject. Indeed he and his chums considered the RE class to be an excuse for a "good carry on" if they could carry it off.

On this particular day, though, it was different. The teacher had promised to talk about Mormonism, as part of a study of "other faiths".

Eric listened to all that was said, contributing to the discussion with a fluency that surprised even himself.

As he reflected later on what he heard that day, little seeds of doubt began to germinate in his mind.

What if this Mormon faith of his wasn't all that it was "cracked up" to be?

But then again, why should he change to anything else? Was there anything else any better? Were all the religions not more-or-less the same?

After all, the Mormons had been very kind to him. He would just stick with them, meantime.

Then one evening his parents said to him as he was setting out to go to a Mormon meeting down at the Mount, "Eric, we don't want you to go back near that Mormon church."

That was funny coming from them. His mum and dad were honest, hard-working, upright folk, but they had never gone overboard about religion.

Making some sort of an excuse that he had "promised" to go tonight, and he couldn't break his promise, Eric went to the meeting.

The seedlings of doubt were beginning to grow in his mind. What was behind this prohibition by his parents?

What was wrong with the Mormons anyway?

It was Billy Douglas, the milkman, who proved to be the greatest influence of all on the spiritual experience of the early teenager. It was with him that Eric worked every morning, and Billy held long chats with his young helper as they drove around.

Billy was a Christian.

He used to listen to Eric explain, as far as he was able, the beliefs of the Mormon faith. Then he would remind the by-now-mildly-muddled Mormon that Jesus Christ did not need to have any special revelation to see God, for He was God in a human form. "God manifest in flesh", was how Billy used to describe it.

Eric liked Billy the person. He had a lot of time of this considerate, caring Christian. The kindness which he showed to his young employee easily matched that of the Mormons. He had a mature contentment about him that Eric admired.

This man was a cut apart. Somebody special somehow.

Although Eric liked Billy the quiet and peaceful man, he definitely didn't like Billy the quietly persistent witness. He had no time whatsoever for the Christian message.

All this talk about being "born again", about being "saved" and about having "new life" in Christ turned him off completely.

It made him angry. Absolutely mad.

So much so that he even considered leaving the job.

Was it not enough for him to keep the commandments, live a good clean life, and mind his own business?

Surely that was enough for anybody?

# CHAPTER THREE

# BIG, SHINY SILVER CUP

IT WAS EARLY OCTOBER, 1962. BILLY DOUGLAS HAD BEEN TO HEAR REV IAN PAISLEY SPEAK IN RAVENHILL FREE PRESBYTERIAN CHURCH, ON THE SUBJECT OF MORMONISM.

This led to the early morning milkrounds becoming daily discussions of the Mormon faith.

"Do you know what the Rev Paisley was talking about last night?" Billy would begin. Then before young Eric had time to reply, and whether he wanted to know or not, he heard!

Billy's recounting of Rev Paisley's observations further increased the doubts in Eric's mind about this religion which he followed so painstakingly.

Rather than seek an alternative right away though, Eric just became all the more angry. He was now spiritually insecure. The rock on which he had placed his faith was gradually but steadily being eroded from below him.

He needed something permanent to trust in. Something which had stood the test of time, having been battered by all the erosive and corrosive agencies of the world.

But where could such a faith be found?

Did it exist?

Eric would have to find out. He needed something. And he needed it soon.

He was thoroughly unhappy.

Although at the age of thirteen he had been baptised into the Mormon faith, yet Eric still continued to attend the Boys Brigade at Everton Drive Mission Hall.

He liked the "BB".

It was great to play games with the other lads and he respected the teacher, Mr Ronnie Carroll. Eric paid little attention to the wee holy bits, as he called them. They weren't for him. Didn't apply.

He was a Mormon, wasn't he?

So he didn't need to listen to that kind of stuff.

One evening, later in the same month, Mr Moore attended a Boys Brigade night. They had only recommenced for a few weeks after the summer recess and Mr Moore was the man with the bright idea for the boys of the Boys Brigade.

It was a bright and shiny idea!

When invited to address the audience of mildly curious lads, Mr Moore produced a big shiny silver cup. The boys were mesmerised and magnetised. Their eyes popped out and their mouths hung open.

They had never seen a silver cup like that one at close quarters before.

TV sports programmes had afforded their only opportunity to briefly glimpse such a gleaming trophy until that very moment. The FA Cup presented at Wembley and other cups presented to golfers and swimmers and the like were things that only happened to rich people far away.

Now here was a man holding one up before their eyes in their own BB hall.

"Like the cup, lads?" Mr Moore asked, knowing from the admiring expressions, what the response would be.

"Yes! Yes! It's lovely!" came the chorus. "Is it for us?"

"It will be for one of you" the benefactor explained.

"This cup is for the member of the Boys Brigade who attends most Sunday nights at our evening service in this hall during the winter months."

There was a general hum of excitement. That would be no problem.

Almost every BB member resolved that he would attend every Sunday service of the winter. What better had they to do on a Sunday night anyway?

Mr Moore was going to have trouble sorting out the winner. He had landed himself with a huge cup-sized problem they reckoned.

Eric was one of the very few who were less than enthusiastic about the whole project. He wasn't going to be conned again.

The young cooling-off Mormon was mightily mixed-up. He was discontent. He was restless.

His adherence to the Mormon creed had kept him occupied by its slavish observance to endless rules, but it hadn't brought any sense of inner peace.

There was always something more to do.

Something higher to achieve.

He could never say that he was finished.

Eric wanted peace and joy and contentment.

He was searching, searching, searching ...

He was prepared to make it abundantly clear when approached, however, that his search wouldn't extend to Everton Drive Mission Hall.

On the way out from the Boys' Brigade that evening, Mr Carroll invited Eric to take part in the come-for-the-cup competition.

"Will you come to the service on Sunday night, Eric?" he enquired warmly. "We would be delighted to see you. Come along with some of the rest of these fellas. They nearly all say they are coming. You never know, you might even win the cup!"

Cup or no cup, Eric Smyth, aged fourteen by now wasn't going to make a long-term commitment of his Sunday evenings.

"OK Mr Carroll," he replied. "I will come this Sunday night. But I want you to know two things. Number one, I am only going to please you, and number two I won't be back! It will be for one night only!"

Having made his point as forcefully as he could, Eric walked out with his friends and they gradually dispersed into the night.

# CHAPTER FOUR

# A NEW CREATION

---

ERIC KEPT HIS PROMISE. WHEN SUNDAY NIGHT CAME HE
WAS SITTING UP AT THE FRONT OF EVERTON DRIVE MISSION
HALL WITH MOST OF THE BOYS BRIGADE COMPANY.

The hall was packed. Everybody appeared glad to see the lads
from the B.B. there.

Great idea, Mr. Moore.

Eric didn't sing the hymns. He didn't know them and he couldn't
read them. The chap beside Eric found the page in the hymn book and
shared his book with him, but Eric just stood in stony silence.

Everyone else seemed to be singing as though it meant something to them. It didn't to him.

When the pastor began to speak it was all about two roads. A
broad road and a narrow road. The broad road led to destruction and the
narrow road led to life.

Gradually Eric heard less and less of what Pastor Hibbert was
talking about. The voice continued but its message was lost on the

thoughtful teenager. He had become totally preoccupied by his own contemplation of the two roads.

"What about the broad road?" came the probing question to his soul. "That's where you are. On the broad road. And destruction. That's where you are going."

God was starting to work in the mind of the confused young man. But he didn't recognise it.

"What about the narrow road?" came the next question. "That's where you need to be. Eternal life. That's what you want, isn't it?"

Eric knew that this was right. He wanted to live forever in heaven, and he recognised that a choice was involved and a change would be necessary.

Difficult things, choices and changes.

Both require backbone.

As the service progressed Eric began to feel scared to look up for he imagined everybody would be staring at him.

He began to feel strangely uncomfortable.

Singled out. Alone. Conspicuous.

How could he possibly feel so isolated in a hall full of people?

After the last hymn had been sung Pastor Hibbert spoke to the hushed congregation.

"I feel that God is working in somebody's life tonight. It could be a young person, or perhaps someone older. If you feel that God is speaking to you, don't put it off. Be saved tonight. Stay behind and talk to me. I will be in the prayer room for some time to come."

With that he sat down quietly, solemnly.

As the congregation filed reverently out, Eric ignored the smiles and nods of his fellow B.B. members. He couldn't understand what was happening to him.

The lad who had consciously made a point of 'switching off' during the 'wee holy bits' on B.B. nights was now possessed by an overwhelming desire to hear more about what he had missed.

He would love to be on the narrow way.

He must get right with God.

"What should I do? Will I stay behind and talk to the pastor? Who will I ask? What will the rest of the lads think of me?"

As he walked slowly down the aisle, touching every seat with his left hand as he passed, Eric's mind was bombarded with questions.

Quick answers would be required.

A courageous choice had to be made.

Having been almost at the front of the Mission Hall that evening, Eric was one of the last to reach the porch. He was hanging back, not wanting to go out, but not sure of what to do.

It was then that he noticed Billy Douglas. There he was, the patently Christian milkman, standing back against a wall.

"Good old Billy," his helper thought. "Here he is again. In the way as usual. When he is the very last person that I want to see, up pops Billy with another spanner in my works."

Although he was unaware of Eric's inward reasonings, Billy could easily observe his dejected appearance.

He stepped forward.

"Do you not think you should get saved tonight, Eric?" he enquired softly. "Would you like to have a chat with the pastor?"

"I would like to talk to somebody," was the muted response.

"All right then, follow me," Billy instructed, leading Eric back up through the by-now-empty hall.

Stopping by a door at the front of the hall, Billy checked that his early-morning assistant had joined him. Then he leaned his head forward towards the door.

When he had satisfied himself that the pastor was alone, Billy knocked the door gently. Then, without waiting for any reply from within, he pushed the door open and ushered the lad forward.

Eric was impressed by his first sighting of the pastor off the platform.

Pastor Will Hibbert was on his knees silently praying for the people to whom he had been speaking ten minutes earlier. There was a sacred serenity about the solitary figure.

When he heard the creak of the door the pastor rose and sat on a chair.

"Eric here would like to talk to you," Billy explained, and then left, closing the door behind him respectfully.

Beckoning with his hand, the pastor directed the subdued lad to a chair beside him.

"And what age are you, Eric?" he asked warmly.

"I'm fourteen," came the brief reply.

"Well, what can I do for you then?" was the pastor's next question.

Eric knew that he wanted somebody to do something for him. He wanted peace instead of turmoil, assurance instead of doubt, but he wasn't sure how to express it.

He didn't speak the language.

"I would like to be on the narrow road," he said at length. "I would like to be sure of eternal life."

"That's good." The pastor was encouraging. "God has made provision for you in Christ Jesus," he replied.

Reaching for the well-worn Bible which lay beside him, the pastor opened it and flicked through a number of pages. As he watched him, Eric was amazed at two things. He had never seen such an obviously-much-used book before, and he was astonished by the way in which the pastor seemed to know what he was looking for amongst its hundreds of pages.

In thirty seconds flat he had turned to the very page that he wanted.

Leaning over beside the fourteen-year-old he pointed to a spot on the page.

"Would you like to read that verse out for me, Eric?" he invited.

The pastor's simple request proved embarrassing to the lad whom he was trying to help.

"I'm sorry, but I can't read," he whispered, apologetically, head down.

"Never mind that," the counsellor continued hastily, "You listen carefully while I read it to you ..."

"For God so loved the world that he gave his only begotten Son, that whosoever believeth in him should not perish, but have everlasting life," was what he read out slowly, deliberately.

After some explanation of John chapter three verse sixteen, Pastor Hibbert said, "Now I'm going to read that verse again, Eric. Listen carefully ..."

"For God so loved Eric Smyth that he gave his only begotten Son that if Eric Smyth believes in him he will not perish but will have everlasting life."

On completing the personalised reading, the pastor enquired, "Do you understand it now, son?"

"Yes I do," replied Eric. "I would like to come to the Lord."

"Well then let's get down on our knees together and we will pray," the experienced counsellor suggested. "You can say a prayer after me. But I want you to pray it from your heart. Don't say these words just because I am asking you to. Pray them because you mean them, and God will answer."

With that he began.

"Come into my heart, Lord Jesus ..."

Then he paused,

"Come into my heart, Lord Jesus," repeated Eric, hesitantly.

"Come in today, come in to stay ..."

Another pause.

"Come in today, come in to stay," repeated Eric. Tears were welling up in his eyes and his voice had begun to tremble.

"Come into my heart Lord Jesus ..."

Pause again. Shorter this time.

"Come into my heart, Lord Jesus," repeated Eric, almost immediately, much more confidently.

It was a genuine invitation to the Saviour. Eric really meant it. The pastor really sensed it.

And the Saviour responded to it in that instant.

Pastor Hibbert placed an arm around the teenager kneeling beside him and thanked God sincerely for saving him.

"Another soul to Jesus born," was a phrase he used.

Young Eric felt so relieved. A tremendous peace flooded into his muddled mind. He felt calmer and more content than he had ever done before in his life.

After a few moments Eric became conscious of the pastor rising stiffly to return to a sitting position. He did the same, but by virtue of his age and agility he was able to execute the manoeuvre much faster.

"God is now your Father, Eric," the pastor advised him, "and you will need to keep in touch with Him. Talk to Him every day in prayer, and read His Word as best you can."

Eric nodded. He would do that.

Such joy, such satisfaction as he felt. It certainly wouldn't be hard to talk to God and thank Him for this wonderful sense of fulfilment, he reckoned.

As they rose to go, with a new Christian setting out to face the world in his newly-found faith, there was something that the pastor considered it essential to warn him about.

"If you never knew there was a Devil before, you will know it tonight, Eric" he cautioned.

Noticing the puzzled look on the lad's face, Pastor Hibbert went on, "There is a verse in Second Corinthians which says, 'If any man be in Christ, he is a new creation. Old things are passed away, behold, all things are become new.'"

The pastor reached for the handle, opened the door, then turned and smiled broadly at Eric.

"You will find that out, too," he said.

~ CHAPTER FIVE ~

# 'THAT'S GOOD SON'

---

WHEN ERIC STEPPED OUT INTO THE NIGHT TO WALK HOME
EVERYONE ELSE HAD GONE. THE PASTOR HAD OFFERED TO
"GIVE HIM A LIFT" BUT HE DECLINED. IT WOULDN'T TAKE
HIM THAT LONG TO WALK HOME AS IT WASN'T VERY FAR.

Anyway, he needed time to think, the pastor's prediction about
the devil had been spot on.

As he walked homewards, Eric's cloudless sky of peace and happiness began to cloud over. Black clouds of doubt and disquiet began to
threaten.

"What are you going to tell the Mormons?" was the first challenge to his composure. "They are going to think that you were some
convert!"

"And what about your mates?" was another ...

Eric had been walking slowly, but even then he wasn't ready to
go into the house. He decided that he would go a very long way round.
Take the scenic route, up the Rocky Road!

This would give him time to ponder. There was so much that he must sort out in his mind.

His mates. He could just hear them

"'Saved' are you now?" they would taunt. "And here's us thought you were a Mormon! Remember the great wee books you used to tell us to read. What kind of a religious nut are you, Smyth?"

Often on that walk up the steep slope of the Rocky Road Eric would stop, turn, and gaze at the city spread out below him. It was a clear night. He could see the shipyard with its cranes, and the massive bulk of the Cave Hill silhouetted against the autumn sky. Lights twinkled all over Belfast. Street lights, flood lights, red lights, head lights ... He could pick them all out.

His mind was awhirl, yes, he was happy. There was a sense of completeness which he had never before experienced.

But what about tomorrow ...?

Never mind tomorrow ... never mind the Mormons ... never mind the mates.

What about tonight? And what about the rest of the family? What would they say?

He was certain that his brothers would laugh at him. There was no doubt about that.

"A Mormon last year. A Christian this year., What will you be next year, Eric?  A Hindu?"

He could anticipate their attitude, their words, their gentle scorn.

As he neared home, the pace slowed to a shuffle.

Eric was determined that he would tell his mother first. Mother had a sympathetic ear for each and every member of the family. She wouldn't laugh at him, he knew that.

Approaching the back door of his home, the fourteen-year-old new-Christian took the pastor's advice. He got in touch with God.

"Please help me, Lord," he prayed silently, fervently.

When he entered the kitchen, his mother was washing dishes at the sink. Eric went out through into the hall, left off his coat, and then rejoined her.

There was no-one else around at that minute and Eric decided to keep it that way if at all possible.

He closed the door into the living room.

What happened next left Ella Smyth dumbfounded. She stared at her son as though he had suddenly gone off his head.

Eric, aged fourteen, picked up a tea-towel and started to dry the dishes that were standing neatly, dripping gently, in the plastic dish drainer.

Mothers know their children. They have an intuitive sixth sense. Mummy Smyth said nothing. This totally uncharacteristic behaviour was a symptom of something.

Could Eric be sick? She wondered. If not, well what had come over him?

Her son was soon to put an end to her mildly curious speculation.

"Mummy, I got saved tonight," he announced, without any pre-amble.

His mother stopped washing the dishes. She rubbed the froth off her right hand with her left one, and then rubbed the froth off her left hand with her right one.

She looked across incredulously at Eric.

He smiled at her. His face glowed.

She smiled back. Her eyes twinkled.

"That's good, son," she said simply.

Ella had never been much of a one for "this getting saved business" as she described it, but she figured that if it could make her rebellious Eric dry the dishes without "a shouting match" it could only be "good"!

There followed an interesting conversation during which Eric first witnessed to his faith in Christ. To his mother.

His forecast of her reactions had been totally accurate.

She had been supportive. Sympathetic to his sincerity, if not completely in sympathy with his salvation.

At least she hadn't laughed at him. But what about his brothers?

Bed time that night proved that he hadn't been mistaken about them either.

Eric shared the biggest bedroom in the house with three of his brothers. Four of them, in two double beds. It was cramped but cosy.

When they were all together in the bedroom, much later in the evening, and during a lull in the getting-read-for-bed banter, Eric announced, "I have something I want to tell you boys."

"And what would that be?" somebody asked.

"I got saved tonight, down in Everton Drive Mission Hall," the new Christian announced, firmly.

The response was almost as Eric had predicted on his Rocky Road ramble.

"Six months," one of them laughed, "we will give you six months."

"O come on now be fair," another brother teased. "How long was he a Mormon? A year, was it? Give him a year!"

Eric smiled at them just as he had done to his mother about an hour and a half before.

He didn't care what they said. All that mattered to him was the tremendous peace in his heart. All the taunts in the world wouldn't deprive him of that.

Then Eric did something which his brothers hadn't seen him do since he was very young.

He slid silently on to his knees at his side of the bed and buried his face in the bedspread. Again he was obeying the pastor's wise counsel. If he was ever going to make his stand for the Lord he would have to start somewhere. And this would be as good a place to begin as any. In his own bedroom with his own brothers.

A hush of respect came over the bedroom as Eric remained on his knees, praying silently.

Chatter either ceased completely or when something had to be said the message was transmitted in a brief, respectful whisper.

The brothers who had been amicably "pulling his leg," admired his courage.

Eric was oblivious to his brothers, tiptoeing about.

He was pouring out his heart to God in praise and prayer.

"Lord Jesus, thank you for coming into my heart and giving me this marvellous peace," he began. "I don't understand it, Lord, but I know that You have something special for me to do. Please Lord, please, show me what."

At that point he paused in his wholly silent prayer in the almost silent room. There was something else to pray about.

His final request was inspired by a burning desire to know more about his God, his Lord and His love, plus hundreds of other mysterious yet marvellous things about the Christian faith. The fulfilment of that desire would be dependent, he knew, at least in some measure, by his success in overcoming his ability to read.

Summarising all his aspirations in one simple supplication, he concluded his prayer with this sincere request, "And Lord, please, somehow, help me to understand Your Book!"

# CHAPTER SIX

# THUMBS UP
# FOR THE BIBLE

IT DIDN'T TAKE LONG FOR THE NEWS TO SPREAD THROUGH
LISNASHARRAGH SECONDARY SCHOOL.

"Did you hear about Eric Smyth?" was the corridor and the cloak-room question nearly every pupil was asking.

If the reply was "No, why, what about him?" then the answer was, "He's turned good livin'. Says he 'got saved' last night."

"But I thought he followed them Mormon boys," somebody was sure to respond.

"Aye, you're right. He did. But he says he has packed that all in. He's a Christian now, or so he says."

This buzz of conversation meant that Eric was a focus of attention at morning break time.

"Tell us this, Eric," some of his friends asked "is it right what they're saying that you have turned good livin'? Again?"

"If you mean that I have got saved then you are right," Eric replied. "I asked the Lord Jesus into my heart last night down in Everton Drive Mission Hall."

Some of them laughed him to scorn.

"Come off it Eric. You're not that type. You will never keep it!" they scoffed.

Others, though, Eric noticed, were less hasty to hassle him. They seemed more thoughtful. Convicted in their own hearts, perhaps, by their friend's courageous witness.

Eric now had a new outlook on life, and a very new spiritual hunger. This led him to start attending the midweek prayer meeting and Bible study group in Everton Drive Mission Hall.

When he started to go at first Eric didn't understand much of what it was all about. One thing he did understand though. These people, most of them much older than he was, were his kind of people. They seemed to have the same ideas, desires and values as he had himself.

It was great to meet with them, and to hear them pray.

How they loved the Lord!

Then a relation of his mother's, John Bentley, arrived unexpectedly at the house one day with a present for Eric. That present was to become Eric Smyth's most prized possession.

It was his first Bible.

Eric carried his new Bible with him to all the services in Everton Drive. Sundays weren't too bad because so many people were present that nobody noticed him, but he felt very self-conscious on a Wednesday night.

Two practical problems began to surface in the life of the new convert. The first was his dyslexia, and the second was a direct result of it. He knew nothing about his beloved Book, and he was finding it difficult to learn, because not only could he not read it, but he could never ever find the place in it when others read it publicly.

This embarrassed him.

Everybody else seemed to have an easy confidence with their Bibles which they produced from pockets and handbags.

Eric felt compelled to conceal his problem and soon developed an effective strategy for doing just that.

When the speaker or study leader announced a Scripture text, the ill-at-ease teenager would join in with the rest, purposefully leafing through the pages.

Then, when the rustling of crinkly paper stopped, and everyone seemed to have found the proper place in the Bible, Eric stopped searching too!

But he had just stopped!

To conceal the fact that he had turned up Mark instead of Micah, or Jonah instead of James he used his thumbs.

Placing a thumb-strategically at the top corner of each page he effectively hid the title of the book. As he gazed intently at the jumble of letters, words and figures on the two pages before him nobody in the congregation ever guessed that he hadn't a clue about what it all meant!

He appreciated so much the friendship which was shown to him in that Mission Hall.

When one service was over he looked forward with eager anticipation to the next.

There was just so much about this wonderful new experience of peace with God to enjoy. And there was so, so much still to learn.

In those early days of his Christian life, as he took his first tottering steps in faith, Eric cherished the quiet encouragement of his father.

A few nights after he was saved, Eric's dad said to him, "Your mum told me that you had come to Christ on Sunday night, son. Is that right?"

Eric was surprised at his father's gentle approach. He had never thought that he would know anything about "coming to Christ".

"Yes, that's right, daddy," Eric replied. "I got saved on Sunday night down in Everton Drive Mission Hall."

"I'm glad, son," his dad responded. And he looked genuinely pleased. Then he went on to explain.

"You see, Eric, when I was about your age or a wee bit older I professed faith in Christ. I was happy for a while and went on well. Then I lost interest in praying and reading my Bible. I fell by the wayside. I really regret it now ..."

As he watched his father's face while he spoke Eric could see that he meant it. A tear glimmered at the corner of his eye.

"You go down to that wee Hall and meet with other Christians. Pray and try to read your Bible. Don't be like me ..."

Turning to go he offered his teenage son his unconditional support.

"And I will help you in any way I can," he volunteered simply.

That promise meant much to Eric.

And it was soon to be put to the test!

Eric had been saved for almost two months when a couple of visitors arrived at the front door, and asked for him,

His father came back into the living-room and said, "There are two Mormons out there wanting to speak to you, Eric. Do you want to talk to them or do you just want me to chase them?!"

"No, don't chase them, daddy. I would need to speak to them," Eric decided.

"Well, all right, on you go then. But don't forget, I'm here if you need me!" father offered.

When Eric went out to the door there stood the two Mormons. Suave, swanky and sweet.

"Nice to see you again, Eric," one of them began in an American accent. "We have missed you down at the Mount recently. We were just wondering if you were ill or something ..."

"No," Eric announced firmly, "I'm not sick, but I have got saved. I won't be going back to the Mormon church."

"Saved, saved, saved" the American repeated. "Saved." What do you mean, "saved"?

Before Eric had time to reply the second Mormon spoke. "I understand what you mean. OK Eric," he said. Eric was pleased to hear that he had a Northern Ireland accent. He would "know the score".

"I know what you mean and I wish you all the best."

Then to Eric's surprise he turned and headed back down the path, leaving his American "missionary" companion with no other available option but to follow!

Left standing open-mouthed on the door-step Eric could only marvel at the mighty power and wisdom of his God!

Before the end of his first year as a Christian two significant thing happened, both of which were a tremendous inspiration to the young convert.

The first was that one of his mates came to know the Lord.

Reggie Humpries was a school-friend of Eric's. He had been one of the more-or-less silent minority who hadn't laughed at him on that stand-up-for-Jesus Monday morning.

Eric spoke to him about his faith, about his peace and happiness, and about the Christian friendship which he had been shown at Everton Drive.

It was a joy for Eric, then, when Reggie accepted his invitation and started to attend the Sunday evening services with him.

Even greater joy was in store, however, when Reggie informed his friend after a service one Sunday evening that he had trusted in the Lord Jesus Christ as his Saviour!

God had answered Eric's sincere but simple prayer ... "Lord, please save Reggie."

The second outstanding event that occurred came as a big but pleasant surprise to the by-now keen-as-mustard Christian. The never-miss-a-meeting Christian.

Eric Smyth, the lad who was only going to please Mr Carroll, and who would definitely only be there for the ONE night, was presented with the cup "for excellent attendance" at Everton Drive throughout the winter!

How pleased he was about that, as well.

These two incidents both encouraged and consoled Eric. They proved to him that although the ability to read appeared to be a pretty useful skill to possess, it was not essential to success, either spiritual or secular.

That was good.

There was hope for him yet!

# CHAPTER SEVEN

# 'OBEY YOUR FATHER AND MOTHER'

WHEN ERIC TURNED FIFTEEN HE LEFT SCHOOL. HE WAS GLAD OF THAT FOR TWO REASONS. THE BURDEN OF LESSONS AND THE CONSTANT EMBARRASSMENT OF BOOKS WAS OVER, BUT MORE IMPORTANTLY, HE HAD FOUND A FULL-TIME JOB IN A MUSHROOM FARM.

He had become a wage-earner! Admittedly not a very big wage-earner. No "fat cat". But a wage-earner nonetheless.

The work on the mushroom farm was enjoyable, different, and the money was useful. The foreman was a Christian who proved to be a source of help and guidance for Eric.

The transition from the governed-by-the-bells-and-books world of school to the more "grown up" world of work couldn't have been easier for him. Or more welcome!

It was also when he was fifteen that he went down to the Free Presbyterian Church on the Ravenhill Road for the first time, to hear Rev Ian Paisley preach.

He sat on the right hand side of the gallery, in the front row. From there he could see and hear everything that went on.

And what he saw and heard impressed him deeply.

The whole atmosphere of the service appealed to the eager teenager. He loved the enthusiastic heart-felt singing of the old-fashioned hymns, and when Rev Paisley began to preach how he relished that.

Eric liked the straightforward approach of the big man in the pulpit. His language was simple, his presentation was forceful, his sincerity was obvious.

When this man preached he seemed to expect God to bless. He had a genuine passion for seeing people brought to Christ.

Eric wasn't long sitting in his gallery seat, soaking up the mood of that meeting, until he had come to a conclusion.

"This is the place for me," he declared. "I want to become a member of this church if I can."

So sure was he that Ravenhill Free Presbyterian Church was where God wanted him to be, that a few months after that first powerful meeting, Eric applied for membership. And was accepted.

It was in his first few weeks in his new church that Eric met Noel Stevenson.

Eric liked Noel. And Noel loved the Lord. He was "on fire for the Saviour".

His face beamed with Christian love as he took a caring interest in this new church-member. It would be important to encourage him, and so Noel invited Eric to join him in open-air witness on summer evenings.

This was, however, long before the days of clip-on fingernail-sized microphones and CD players!

The two young men would board the bus outside the church on a sunny evening loaded down with their gear.

One of them carried the big heavy 12-volt battery which powered the PA system, and the microphone. The other lugged along the wind-up gramophone and the bag of "78" records.

Each of them carried his Bible.

On arrival at their destination which could have been somewhere in the Downshire estate, or up the Cregagh Road, or the Ravenhill Road or the Woodstock Road, they assembled their equipment.

After adjusting the microphone to stop it whistling and whining they wound up the gramophone and played a few records. When a number of people gathered around them, whether out of interest or mere curiosity it mattered little, Noel and Eric took turns to speak.

They adopted the direct methods of their minister, simply telling the bystanders what God had done in each of their lives, and what He could still do for those who trusted in Christ.

Noel Stevenson gave valuable support to Eric in his early days in Ravenhill Free Presbyterian Church. He showed the young convert how he could fulfil his growing desire to reach others for Christ, by getting out on to the streets and into the estates and witnessing to them.

It was also in that church, when still in his mid-teens that Eric learned the importance of sustained and earnest prayer.

Here he met people who really wanted to pour out their hearts to God. They believed that He would answer their prayers because they were His children.

Eric enjoyed the prayer times so much that he began to attend the all-night prayer meetings in the church on a Friday night.

He had never thought it possible that busy men and women could come together after a day's work and stay awake to pray all night. But these people did.

Eager Eric joined them for a few weeks, leaving the meeting before it finished to catch the early bus on to his work on the mushroom farm at 7.00am on Saturday morning.

A conflict of interests soon developed.

It was obvious that Eric's parents were not happy with his attendance at the meeting all night and then setting off to his work without any sleep.

"After all, Eric son, you are only fifteen," they pointed out.

Eric, however, had decided that by going to the prayer meeting he "was putting God first", and hadn't he heard somewhere that it said in the Bible that he ought to "obey God rather than man".

Surely that applied even if the man was you own father. Or did it?

There was only one way to sort the whole matter out, he reckoned. He could ask Rev Ian Paisley, who was undoubtedly a man of God. He would give him the right advice.

One night after a service Eric recounted the delicate situation to the minister whom he very much revered, highlighting particularly the conflict of concerns that was tearing him apart.

His burning desire to attend the all-night prayer meeting.

His parents' understandable anxiety for the health and safety of their fifteen-year-old son.

It didn't take many minutes for Rev Paisley to give his verdict on the subject. Eric was just a little surprised that he didn't take more time to weigh up the "pros-and-cons" of the matter.

"Son, obey your father and mother!" was his almost instantaneous counsel.

Noticing the disappointment on Eric's face when he paused, he then went on, "See if they would allow you to come until 11.30pm. Then you could go home to bed."

When Eric put this proposition to his parents later on in the evening they were completely happy with it. And he was happy that they were happy.

He wasn't going to miss out on the prayer meeting either as he was going to be able to attend for a few hours each Friday evening.

"Son, obey your father and mother."

It was sound advice.

# CHAPTER EIGHT

# 'I LOVE YOU!'

THE CITY HALL IS AT THE HUB OF BELFAST. ROADS RADIATE FROM IT SPOKE-LIKE.

In the early 1960's the roads and streets around that impressive building were the location for a variety of open-air services, especially at the weekends. Evangelical groups of subtly differing shades of theological opinion congregated there to sing and preach the gospel.

Eric loved to go down to the city centre "to the open airs".

It was great to hear so many earnest people proclaiming "The Message" as he called it. There was an added bonus to the open-airs as well, in the fact that a number of attractive teenage girls seemed to have similar interests to himself!

Young Christian people from all parts of Belfast seemed to converge on the City Hall, as though drawn by some giant magnet.

One Sunday evening after an open-air service, Eric was introduced to Frances Swaffield from Sandy Row. He took an instant liking to the girl. Dark hair, warm smile, a Christian.

After a few weeks of watching her, gauging her reactions to him, wondering should I? Shouldn't I? When will I? approach her, hoping for a positive response - Eric took the plunge.

He asked her out.

Frances was only too pleased to accept. She had begun to think that he was never going to get round to asking! She had been watching the glint in his eye for those few weeks also!

They both enjoyed each other's company. Met regularly "at the open airs". Then started to attend each others' churches.

The more often they met the happier they were. The time they spent together grew longer and longer and the interval between their meetings grew shorter and shorter.

Eric was so happy to have a girl-friend who loved the Lord like he did. Somebody to talk to, have a meal with, walk home with on the late-night city streets.

An intense bond of affection began to develop between the two young people.

After six months they decided that they wanted to spend the rest of their lives together.

So they were engaged to be married.

Although the engagement brought great excitement and anticipation to the young couple it caused some concern to their parents.

"You are far too young to be getting married, Eric" his parents told him a number of times after Frances and he had announced their engagement. "You would be far better to wait a year or two," they advised. "Gather up some money. It takes money to run a home, you know."

Underlying the voiced concerns of his parents was the       consciousness of Eric's dyslexia. How could a young man , aged seventeen-and-a-half, who could neither read nor write, manage a home? They were really worried.

Despite the parental misgivings, Eric and Frances proceeded with their plans.

They were "meant for each other". They just knew it!

The wedding date was set for 10th September, 1966. The venue was to be Ravenhill Free Presbyterian Church. The officiating minister was to be Rev Ian Paisley.

All the plans were made well in advance. Everything was "cut-and-dried". They just couldn't wait for "the big day".

Then the hitches began.

Number one, the boat strike. During the summer of 1966 there was a shipping strike and shortages began to occur. As the transportation of essentials took priority the movement of luxuries stopped.

One of the luxuries that ended up in short supply were wedding dresses! And Frances couldn't afford to have one made.

What would the bride-to-be do?

Then came hitch number two. The imprisonment of Rev Ian Paisley. Eric was very disappointed about this. He had so looked forward to having his special spiritual mentor performing their wedding ceremony...

What would the groom-to-be do?

When Saturday, 10th September came, both families turned out, dressed in their finery, to witness the marriage of Eric and Frances.

Problems which had caused anxiety in the preceding months vanished away like the early morning mist on the River Lagan.

Rev John Douglas performed the ceremony so graciously and Frances looked striking in a pink suit.

The deep affection that was shared by the young couple became very evident to those within earshot in the church, as they walked down the aisle, Mr and Mrs Eric Smyth.

The groom had been looking around, nodding and smiling to his friends. Suddenly Frances tugged at the arm she was linked on. When her husband-of-twenty-minutes looked round to see what she wanted, she was smiling broadly, glowing happily.

"I love you!" she whispered.

The reception was held across the city in Emmanuel Mission Hall on Sandy Row. Eric and Frances had a lot of love to share, a lot of plans to make, but not a lot of money to spend.

They couldn't afford a fancy hotel reception!

Their friends in Frances' home church came to their aid and arranged a marvellous reception for them.

Everybody enjoyed that.

It hadn't been an expensive reception. But it didn't matter to the newly weds. It had been a warm and friendly one. And they were so happy.

There was no such thing as a continental or Caribbean honeymoon for them either. The honeymoon was spent for a week in Portrush.But it didn't matter to the newly-weds. They were just so glad to be with each other. All the time.

The summer stir had died away from the north-coast resort in mid-September.

Half-deserted amusement arcades held no appeal for them.

They chatted eagerly about their future life together as they walked in the bracing wind around Ramore Head.

They laughed gleefully together when the wind scudded the sand against their ankles as they laboured along the East Strand to the White Rocks.

It was marvellous. What a wonderful week!

They had to come home.

They didn't mind that, though, for it was to their own rented house in Norwood Street, off Sandy Row.

Two rooms up.

Two rooms down.

Two contented people inside.

Now they were all set to start out in life together.

In earnest.

In Christ.

# CHAPTER NINE

# FAMILY MAN, MICHELIN MAN

A WELCOME SURPRISE AWAITED ERIC WHEN HE RETURNED TO HIS WORK IN THE MUSHROOM FARM.

The foreman informed him that since he was 'a conscientious employee' and 'now a married man,' he had been promoted to 'charge hand'.

In recognition of his promotion his weekly wage would be increased to ten guineas.

This was real promotion! Imagine, ten guineas!

Just over a year after their wedding Eric and Frances received the best bonus they could possibly have expected.

It was the birth of their first child, a daughter, Karen.

What joy and delight the little one brought to the young couple!

What responsibility she brought with her too!

Eric Smyth was not only Christian, husband, breadwinner, but now he was father as well!

As their baby daughter grew, almost her every move, stretch and burble was monitored by her adoring parents, watching for 'progress'.

This sense of belonging to each other, and their baby daughter, deepened with the passing days.

Eric and Frances were very conscious, not only of their love for each other, but also of their love for the Lord. They wanted to live for him. To please Him. To honour Him in their daily lives.

In this respect Eric began to see an ambition taking one baby-step towards realisation, his prayer showing hopeful sings of being answered.

He found that with persistence there were certain oft-recurring Scriptural word patterns that he could recognise.

His experience with the printed word could not yet accurately be described as 'reading', but he was beginning to be able to piece together enough to allow him to understand a little.

A very little. He was encouraged and heartened by this.

When they discovered that they were expecting to double their family, Eric and Frances realised that their tiny house in Norwood Street would be totally inadequate.

Apart from the fact that their four rooms were all small, they didn't have a bathroom.

And their only toilet was 'in the yard'.

However delighted Eric had once been to receive his promotion and his wage of ten guineas, now with one child present and another pending, he recognised that it wouldn't be enough. They couldn't 'make ends meet.'

A change of job would be welcome.

And so would a change of house.

Moves were called for.

And came.

When they were told that they had been allocated a maisonette in the Glencairn estate off Ballygomartin Road in the Shankill area of the city, the young parents were delighted.

It would be a more modern dwelling than the one in Norwood Street. A larger house for an expanding family.

And they would have a bathroom. Plus an inside toilet. Great!

They flitted with great enthusiasm, early in 1968. The chilling-damp or the frosty-crisp of January and February didn't worry them.

They were so pleased with their new, comfortable home, and so occupied with furnishing it.

A few months after they had moved in, Eric junior was born.

Now they had one of each.

Another little perfect creation to watch, and wonder at.

Another little mouth to feed.

With the constant demand of an increased rent, and the varied demands of an increasing family, more money was desperately needed.

Eric's parents had been right. "It takes money to run a home, you know!" Words of wisdom, once disregarded, were now proving to be true.

After some searching around and a number of applications to various prospective employers, Eric was appointed to a job in the Michelin tyre factory in Mallusk.

It was in that factory that the new employee found, somewhat to his surprise, at first, that it was possibly to be persecuted for doing your job well.

Eric was a tyre checker. He was responsible for scrutinising the finished tyres for faults before they left the factory. Other men had the same task.

In this particular job, Eric's disability, actually helped him. Since he couldn't read instruction booklets, or even labels, Eric devised his own method of checking the brand-new tyres. When his workmates realised that his method of doing the job was quicker and more effective than the standard practice, they were not amused.

They didn't like this ultra hard-working, a-day's-work-for-a-day's-pay, conscientious Christian type.

He was getting through more work than they were, yet he was checking every single tyre. No skips. None thrown 'over the machine.'

One day a director of Michelin came around to visit the factory floor. Everybody was expected to be working his best. Showing the place off to its full advantage.

Eric was working away diligently, with his New Testament propped up on his machine, as usual. Since making the discovery that he could  recognise certain patterns in the words of the Bible, Eric kept his pocket New Testament with him all the time.

On the machine at work it served a dual purpose.

It was both a source of inspiration, and a flagship of his faith.

A foreman was conducting 'the big noise', a Frenchman, on his tour of the factory.

The Frenchman's eyes rested on the opened New Testament.

"This man ... this man ... this book ... this machine," he began, all hands and mouth and eyes. He stumbled over his English out of frustration.

The foreman looked at Eric, and at the book and then at the gesticulating Frenchman. Then he smiled.

"What is this man doing?" the boss-man became more articulate as he became more controlled. "For what is this book on his machine?"

"I don't know what effect the book on his machine has on him, " the foreman replied, "but it certainly must help him. He is one of my best workers."

It was Eric's turn to smile quietly to himself as the Frenchman blustered hurriedly on.

Somebody had noticed his diligence.

He had proved himself to be what his cherished New Testament described as a 'workman with no need to be ashamed.'

# CHAPTER TEN

# BEAUTIFUL FEET

---

ERIC THE MICHELIN MAN NEEDED A CAR. PUBLIC TRANS-
PORT FROM THE SHANKILL ROAD TO THE FACTORY AT
MALLUSK WAS AVAILABLE DURING THE DAY, BUT NON-EX-
ISTENT AT NIGHT.

So he bought himself a second-hand car. It was a Ford Cortina.
The old nineteen-sixties model, all square shapes and sharp edges.

There was one feature about this particular vehicle that the seller
just somehow seemed to omit to mention to Eric when he purchased it.

The car was a dry-weather model. It didn't like the wet. When its
plugs and points got the slightest whiff of damp they lost their spark.
And flatly refused to function!

Eric became used to its eccentricities.

One wet, windy night he left the house to go to work, really only
half-expecting to make it.

When he had jumped into the driver's seat, he closed the door
again hastily after him.

Rain was blowing in everywhere.

He knew it would be up in the works!

Hopefully, he turned the key in the ignition. Nothing but the metallic gurr-gurr of the starter turning over.

No life.

After a number of attempts, the metallic gurr-gurr of the starter turning over changed to the slow, painful gurrrr... of the battery running down.

Better give it up. There would be no work tonight.

Eric retraced his steps into the house.

Frances greeted him with, "I thought you would be back!"

"So did I!" Eric admitted. "Why can the car people not make cars that will go on wet nights?"

His wife noted to herself, however, that it probably was not an issue that he was going to make a lot of fuss about. He didn't appear to be all that terribly upset that he wasn't going to be able to make it to his work.

When he had phoned his employers to inform them that he wouldn't be in, for 'the car wouldn't start,' Eric didn't feel like going to bed. He had been on his way to work and was wide awake.

What would he do with himself?

No problem.

He settled down to spend a hour or two doing something which was rapidly becoming a tremendous source of pleasure to him.

Poring over his Bible. Actually making sense of it.

He had become more expert at finding the place. With constant practice he had also learned to read less laboriously.

He had tremendous motivation.

All he wanted to do was learn more and more about his Saviour and His love, His teachings in His Book.

When the family had all retired to bed, Eric sat on an armchair by the fire, flicking through his Bible.

The rain beat incessantly on the window. Eric barely heard it. He was so preoccupied with the Scripture.

He had turned to Romans chapter ten. As he read down the verses, slowly, painstakingly, he was arrested by verse fourteen. It expressed much of what Eric had been thinking about in the previous few months.

He was concerned for the spiritual welfare of the people who lived around him. In Cairnmartin and on the Shankill Road.

There seemed to be thousands of people, thronging about from day to day, but they didn't know about, or at least they didn't seem to care about, his Lord, and the happiness and peace that only He could bring.

Eric felt that he had to tell them. He must.

The words of the verse struck home to his heart.

"How then shall they call on him in whom they have not believed? and how shall they believe in him of whom they have not heard? And how shall they hear without a preacher?"

A preacher. That was the answer.

"How shall they hear without a preacher?"

But then again, Eric mused, they have a preacher. They don't hear him though. They don't want to hear him.

His mind focused on the John Knox Memorial Church in Clifton Park Avenue where he went every Sunday. A beautiful building. Very attractive architecturally.

There was a preacher in there. A good one too. And he wasn't by any means the only one. There were others. Sincere men who preached the Gospel every Sunday, usually to congregations largely comprised of Christians.

There must be some other way of preaching, Eric concluded. Surely there must be some way in which his neighbours could hear 'a preacher.'

His Bible had slid down his knee, and his restraining hand had crumpled the page. Flattening out the crumpled page, Eric looked again at verse fifteen.

He read it over and over three times.

His dyslexia meant that the snail's pace of his deliberate reading allowed him to grasp the meaning more readily.

There was something in there which he had never noticed before, 'How beautiful are the feet of them that preach the gospel of peace'

'The feet,' it said. 'How beautiful are the feet of them that preach the gospel of peace'

It didn't say 'the mouth of the preacher.'

It clearly stated, 'How beautiful are the FEET.'

Suddenly a tremendous truth dawned upon the would-be-witness as he sat by the dying fire.

You didn't necessarily have to be eloquent to be an effective preacher. You did, however, have to be prepared to be active. To use your 'feet'.

This was something which Eric could do. He could walk around his neighbours and talk the gospel to them. Show them love and concern, treat them with grace and kindness and tell them about his Saviour. Door-to-door, one-to-one, or one-to-two or three, personal evangelism.

He couldn't preach from the pulpit because of his lack of education; but he could walk around and contact the people in the district. What Eric lacked in education he more than made up for in dedication and fervent desire.

This was it.

A few nights later he put his idea into practice. He started out, on his feet, to call with his neighbours and tell them about Jesus.

It began in a small way. Just one evening per week.

Eric soon realised that this was what God wanted him to do. This was preaching. Different from the Sunday-morning-in-the-pulpit variety no doubt, but preaching nonetheless.

Some people showed a genuine interest in the simple message from the Bible that their earnest neighbour explained. The good news of salvation through the death of Christ.

They invited Eric to return and tell them more. This he gladly did.

Soon his one night a week became two. Out on the streets telling people about the Saviour.

There were times when Frances felt like asking, "Do you not think Eric that you should stay at home tonight and help me with the children?"

It was perhaps with some justification that she could have asked such a question. The children were increasing in number. Mark, their third child, was just a baby. Karen and Eric were growing bigger and becoming more demanding, yet she refrained.

This was God's work. Eric was happy in it. A few souls had come to a living personal faith in Jesus Christ.

Who was she to question?

# CHAPTER ELEVEN

# PLEASE HELP ME!

---

INCREASED FAMILY DEMANDS BROUGHT WITH THEM IN-
CREASED FINANCIAL DEMANDS.

The expanding family needed more accommodation. So they
moved to a bigger house in the Ballysillan area of Belfast. This in its
turn meant an increase in rent.

Eric needed more pay. He needed another job. When the opportunity arose he applied for one. On the security gates in the city centre.

The escalating troubles in the early nineteen seventies had led to
the erection of security gates at all access points to the main shopping
precincts. These gates had to be manned both day and night. Greater
numbers of personnel had to be recruited to meet these requirements.

Eric was invited to present himself for interview in River House,
High Street, Belfast.

When he duly attended he was shown into a room where eight
other people were waiting.

There was a polite, edgy silence.

When a gentleman emerged from an office somewhere, with a folder full of papers the tension eased a little.

Something was about to happen!

Action at last!

The relaxation in tension was only a momentary experience for Eric, however.

When the man with the folder started distributing forms to the waiting nine, his face turned pale and his legs went weak.

The natural suspense of anticipation gave way to an unnatural but perhaps understandable sense of blind panic.

The form was a straightforward enough document asking for basic information. Name? Address? Date of birth? Marital status? Details of present and previous employment …

Eric went to pieces.

A cold sweat came over him.

He considered dashing to the door and beating a hasty retreat.

Then he thought of the money.

It was good, and he needed it.

As he studied the form more intently than it ever deserved, an idea came into his mind.

He began to work out a plan. There was a way out of this fix. If only somebody would help him …

Eric pretended to read his form until the chap beside him had his completed. Then he leaned over and whispered, "I wonder if you could help me here, mate. I can't read very well and I can't spell at all. So I can't fill this thing in. If I tell you the stuff will you write it down for me?"

The young man smiled. His face was a picture. A countenance depicting both mild amazement and mild amusement in the self-same expression.

Thankfully he was helpful.

"OK. No problem," he replied.

Hurriedly, and almost under his breath, Eric gave an answer to each question as his press-ganged assistant read them out, one by one.

Soon it was finished.

"Can you sign your name?" his helper enquired.

Now it was Eric's turn to smile.

"Oh aye. I can do that OK!" Eric assured him.

And he did. On the line that his friend-in-need pointed to, the one with the hastily-scribbled x beside it, at the bottom of the page.

"Thanks mate. That was very kind of you."

Eric was genuinely grateful.

When all the forms had been collected again, and he had been interviewed, Eric went home to wait for the results of his application.

And he waited. And waited. And waited ...

As time passed, and pressing problems took priority he began to forget about it. On the becoming-fewer occasions when it did cross his mind he instantly dismissed it.

Put it down to experience.

Just yet another lost cause.

Imagine his surprise and delight then, when almost three months later he received a letter informing him that he had been appointed as an attendant on the security gates.

He was to commence duties on the first day of the next month.

Eric enjoyed those early days on the security gates. They were happy, fulfilled and rewarding. They were also a challenge. Especially to somebody who couldn't read!

He was often forced to spell out the details of a licence into his two-way radio, while an impatient motorist waited at the gate. Some of the handwriting in those old licences was barely legible for the literate, thus creating a desperate dilemma for the dyslexic.

Eric discovered that a number of his workmates in his new position were Christians. Joe Haveron, David McAniney, George Birnie and David Beck were all a tremendous help to him. And he to them when he could. They used to have lively Bible studies in the lunch-break, when they shared with and helped each other.

An amazing number of people passed through those gates. At busy periods the queue to enter the shopping precinct was often five metres long.

One cold, crisp early November day, late in the afternoon Eric was working away as usual. Belfast was busy. Buzzing.

Despite the ongoing "troubles" people were wrapping up and stepping out ...

The thought struck Eric like a thunderbolt ... Hundreds of people. Decent people. Without Christ.

These fellow-citizens of his were so busy with their own affairs, so interested in keeping their bodies warm and safe, that they didn't ever give the slightest consideration to the safety and security of their souls.

They didn't know Christ as Saviour. And what was worse, it didn't seem to bother them one bit.

Eric couldn't get the thought out of his mind.

Hundreds of patient people slowing up to be checked, then dashing on about their business. To where? To what, eventually?

It was late when he arrived home that evening. His shift didn't end until eleven o'clock. It was just after eleven-thirty when he made it to the house. The family were all in bed.

Eric took off his coat and threw it down on the settee in the living room.

Then he threw himself down beside it.

People. Lots of them. Dozens, scores, hundreds of them without a Saviour.

What should be done?

What could be done?

What could he, just one among so many do?

In frustration of spiritual anxiety, he reached across to the sideboard and lifted his Bible. He began to flick through its pages.

Eric had never been one to go in much for verses-at-random. Verses-at-all were usually quite an achievement for him.

On this occasion, however, he was searching for comfort. For guidance. For help.

The fluttering pages came to rest, leaving the Bible open at the book of Jeremiah, chapter eighteen.

Eric began to read, slowly.

It was about a potter, his wheel, and clay. Marred pots and patient moulding. A vivid description.

The message of verse six was addressed to "the house of Israel" but Eric applied it to himself.

"O house of Israel, cannot I do with you as this potter? saith the Lord. Behold as the clay is in the potter's hand, so are ye in mine hand, O house of Israel" he read silently.

"As the clay is in the potter's hand, so are you in my hand ..."

Those words jogged Eric's memory. His thoughts travelled back to the old gramophone at the open airs with Noel Stevenson. And the 78s. There was one called "Have Thine Own Way". He struggled to remember the words.

Gradually they came back to him.

"Have Thine own way, Lord,
Have Thine own way,
Thou art the potter,
I am the clay.
Mould me and make me,
After Thy will.
While I am waiting,
Yielded and still."

Eric was moved.

For years now he had been making excuses for himself.

"I can't read, so I can't learn. I can't learn, so I can't go to Bible College. I can't go to Bible College so I can't be a preacher. There isn't an awful lot I can do, really."

Then he recalled the experience of Glencairn. The "beautiful feet" of the preacher. The souls he had been able to talk to, and lead to the Lord.

There was no valid excuse whatsoever.

His problem was an over emphasis on his own inability and an underestimate of God's capability.

He cried out in agony of soul.

Eric had come to the point where he was willing to submit himself, body, soul and mind to God. To do with as HE pleased.

It was well after midnight when he changed his position. When he had moved from sitting on the settee to kneeling at it Eric prayed aloud. Earnestly. Fervently.

"Lord, what do you want me to do? I will do anything that I can for You. Anything You want me to. Show me Your way. Your will, Lord. Please help me ..."

By now his body was stretched at an angle across the seat of the settee. With chin resting on his folded arms, he remained motionless, silent.

It was then that God spoke to him.

"Leave it all to me," He seemed to say. "Let Me mould you and make you. Let Me lead you and guide you. Stop worrying about what you can or cannot do. Just trust yourself to me. I can, and will help you. I can do anything, everything. And I can make something out of you as well ..."

Eric rose from his knees and hung up his jacket and overcoat.

Then he went to bed and slept soundly.

The clay was in the hands of the Master Potter.

The Lord was in control.

~ CHAPTER TWELVE~

# ARE YOU CRAZY,
# OR WHAT?

---

ERIC WAS NOW DEDICATED TO THE LORD. HE WANTED TO GO INTO FULL-TIME SERVICE FOR HIS MASTER.

But how could he? Was it really feasible?

After spending two years in the house in Ballysillan, the family moved back to Forth River Parade in the Glencairn area of the Shankill Road in February 1972.

Following that move, during the mid-seventies, Eric worked away at the security gates during the day and busied himself with door-to-door visitation in his off-duty periods.

He longed to be free to spend every hour of every day contacting people for Christ.

Frances didn't share his burning desire, though.

She had a much more pragmatic approach to the whole situation. She tried "to talks sense into" her husband.

"Eric, I know you want to serve the Lord full-time," she would say. "But look at it this way. God has given us six children. Six little mouths to feed. Six little bodies to clothe. Isn't that responsibility enough?"

She referred to the fact that in the intervening years Keith, Andrew and Jonathan had been born, brothers to Karen Eric and Mark.

Six of them! And her husband was talking about leaving his job!

Frances fully appreciated Eric's desire to see souls saved. She had the same ambition herself. It just wasn't sensible, she thought, to expect a man to provide for a wife and six growing children, without any regular source of income.

Eric was acutely aware of his wife's concern. A mother's love and practical care for her family were understandable.

But still he was absolutely convinced that God was calling him into all-day-every-day Christian work.

What should he do?

He took the only course of action open to him.

He prayed.

Early in 1978 Eric committed the matter to God in prayer. God had told him all those years ago that He would use him. Now Eric was becoming impatient for action.

He yearned to be involved in some aspect of full-time Christian ministry. But he wouldn't proceed into anything without his wife's wholehearted support. That would be vital.

"Right Lord," he prayed one evening. "I want to serve You, and You know that, but I'm not moving until you show Frances the way."

Having left the issue with God, Eric resigned himself to awaiting His time.

The waiting was hard. He was straining on the leash. Rarin' to go.

His mounting impatience led to him becoming unsettled at his daytime job. The crowds still thronged through the gates and he still saw them through the eyes of his Saviour.

"He had compassion on them."

How he hankered to be free to tell them of Him, and His dying love for them.

Then, totally unexpectedly, Eric had a telephone call from Frances one day at lunch-time.

When mother had answered all of father's "What-about-the-kids?" type questions, she came around to the real purpose of her call.

"I just thought I would let you know, Eric, that God has been speaking to me this morning through that verse in Ecclesiastes chapter eleven, 'Cast thy bread upon the waters: for thou shalt find it after many days.' You know that I have been doubtful about you going into full-time service for the Lord for a number of years now. Well, I'm not going to stand in you way any longer. If you want to leave your job there and concentrate on Christian work, I'm right behind you. God will look after us."

Eric was taken unawares. Shocked into silence.

When he recovered his voice it was only to ask incredulously, "You don't really mean it Frances, do you?"

"Yes. I do, love. I mean it," came the calm and confident response.

"Thanks dear. Thanks," Eric went on. "Must go now. We will talk it all over together tonight."

When he had put the receiver down Eric sat stock-still. He stared at the silent telephone. Had he been hearing right?

Yes. He had. No doubt about it.

A sense of calm, of peace, of being in the mind and will of God flooded his soul.

It had been over a year since he had asked God to "show Frances the way". And he hadn't mentioned his calling to full-time work to her from that day.

It had become "a touchy subject" between them.

Now that God in His great wisdom and in His own time had granted his request, Eric just had to express his appreciation.

"Thank you, God, for answering my prayer," he whispered reverently, before returning to the afternoon shift. "Thank you for bringing Frances to this point. Please lead us both on from here."

On arriving home after work, he was delighted to discover that Frances was as resolute as she had been at lunch-time. She hadn't changed her mind. God had revealed Himself, His power and His ability to provide, to her, in a very definite way. She reassured Eric repeatedly, in the course of that evening, that she would be firmly behind him, if that was what God was calling him to do.

After sustained thought and prayer Eric went to discuss the matter with Rev David Crane, minister of John Knox Memorial Free Presbyterian Church. He was very helpful and encouraged Eric to enter full-time Christian work.

As they chatted together at length Rev Crane recognised two things. He was convinced of the definite nature of Eric's call to service, and he had been aware for some time of the positive impact his "beautiful feet" door-to-door personal ministry.

There was a mixed reaction when Eric announced to his friends on the security gates that he was leaving his job, to concentrate on full-time Gospel work.

Some encouraged him, knowing the depth of his Christian commitment, whilst others, including some in the "God-squad", as they had become good-naturedly nicknamed, were more cautious.

"Do you think this is wise, Eric?" they would counsel. "We know about 'being out in faith' and all that kind of thing, but do you think you can cope? Remember, you have a wife and six kids to look after."

"No boys. I don't think I can cope. On my own that is. But I know God can, and He has promised both Frances and me that He will look after us. That is all I have to go on," was their workmate's simple counter to their well-intentioned concern.

Although he kept up this brave face in public, there were times when Eric had his own doubts, too. On the face of it, from a purely human point of view, it seemed a crazy idea. No wonder some people had their reservations. In his quiet moments he had them occasionally himself.

When misgivings seemed to clog his mind, he always returned in thought to Romans chapter ten and Jeremiah chapter eighteen.

"How beautiful are the feet of them that preach the gospel of peace, and bring glad tidings of good things ..."

"Cannot I do with you as this potter? saith the Lord. Behold, as the clay is in the potter's hand, so are ye in mine hand ..."

Meditation on these texts never failed to unclog the system.

Through these verses God had called him.

Surely the Almighty God who had led him thus far, had still sufficient resources of wisdom, knowledge and power to steer him safely into the future.

So it was that in May, 1979, Eric Smyth took the bold step and left full-time employment to enter Christian work. This would allow him to concentrate on what he loved to do so much. Visiting people in their homes. Helping them where he could. And always telling them of Christ and His everlasting love for all mankind.

He was supported by voluntary donations from members of his church and other interested Christian friends.

Sometimes it was tough.

There were weeks when the family lived on the Family Allowance. Yet the God who called, proved Himself faithful.

Whenever there was a need, it was met. And only God, in prayer, had been told about it.

In June 1979 Eric applied to enter the Whitefield College of the Bible, and was accepted to commence studies in October.

Throughout the summer months Eric was happy and busy on the city streets. Talking to friends and neighbours. Pointing them to the Lord.

As the summer progressed and the number of letters landing on the hall mat from the Whitefield College of the Bible began to increase, Eric realised that it was not the place for him.

There were lists of recommended books to buy, recommended reading lists, and an outline of the various subject elements in each term's study schedule.

No doubt hundreds of people benefit from a Bible College education, but Eric Smyth, the dyslexic who left school unable to read or write recognised that it wasn't his scene. He just couldn't manage it. It would be like going back to school again and that certainly wasn't something that he ever wanted to do!

So Eric cancelled his application and carried on doing what he found so rewarding.

Walking, talking, presenting Christ.

God began to bless his work.

God continued to provide for his family.

And God had more, much more, in store for him.

# CHAPTER THIRTEEN

# COUNCILLOR SMYTH

---

ERIC SMYTH HAD ALWAYS BELIEVED THAT FOR MORAL AND SOCIAL REASONS CHRISTIANS SHOULD BE INVOLVED IN LOCAL POLITICS.

This conviction was confirmed to him as he went around the doors, talking to the people.

Shortly after leaving his employment on the security gates, Eric took charge of a little outreach Mission Hall in Aughrim Street, in the Sandy Row area of Belfast. There were a limited number of services in the Hall, mainly on Sunday evenings and a few on winter weeknights.

As he contacted the local residents, inviting them to the services and talking to them about the Gospel, he realised that they were genuinely interested in, and concerned about, more mundane matters. Like the state of the footpaths, the inadequacy of the street lighting and the lack of basic heating and sanitary facilities in their homes.

When Councillor Billy Dixon of the Donegall Road Ward asked Eric, then, in January 1981, to stand as a candidate for the May elections to the City Council he gave it careful consideration.

If elected this would allow him to put his beliefs into practice. Channel his energies into representing the people of the Donegall Road and Sandy Row areas of Belfast, in the City Hall. And it would also provide him with the opportunity to uphold the Christian ethic in a society which he considered to be on a slippery slope, sliding gaily away from God and His standards.

When he had prayed about it for some time, and asked advice from a number of his closest friends, Eric decided to allow his name to be put forward as a DUP candidate in the election.

Then the hard work began.

Door-to-door canvassing.

Planning and policy meetings.

Early mornings and late nights.

Eric was experienced in meeting the people. On their doorsteps, in their living-rooms. He had been doing it for years. Now he had the chance to demonstrate to the residents of the ward that he was concerned for their physical as well as their spiritual welfare.

There were many invitations into the homes of these sincere, down-to-earth people. Eric Smyth, the homely man, the family man, the Christian man, took the time to listen to them as they chatted by their firesides. And he talked to them ...

Advising. Counselling. Reassuring.

One evening on the campaign trail on the Donegall Road, an elderly man invited Eric into his home. In conversation, the would-be councillor realised that this man needed more than a street-light outside his door.

The darkness was in his life. There was a gaping void of discontent, deep in the heart of him. He was craving for something, but he knew not what.

As they talked he wiped away silent tears with the ragged cuff of his well-worn woollen cardigan.

Eric spent almost two hours with that old man. What did a few more votes matter now? This was a life-or-death-for-eternity matter, he reckoned.

Before he left that home that evening Eric had pointed his could-be-constituent to Christ. And left him happy. Rejoicing. At peace with himself and God.

What an encouragement!

And there were times when he needed encouragement.

There were always those to criticise. To cast doubts on the ability of a dyslexic, out-of-work security man and part-time "Bible-thumper" to represent them on the City Council.

"What does he know about anything?" they would ask with a smirk. "Sure he can't even write, the man."

His political opponents didn't exactly smother him with kindness and understanding either.

The unswerving support of his wife, his friends in church and in the Democratic Unionist Party, meant a lot to him in those busy spring days.

His greatest source of comfort, though, was in God, and in His promise to lead him, guide him, help him, mould him.

Late one evening as he read his Bible, Eric discovered Jeremiah chapter one, verse nineteen.

It proved to be just the kind of pledge he needed.

It was an Omnipotent God speaking. He said, "And they shall fight against thee; but they shall not prevail against thee: for I am with thee, saith the Lord, to deliver thee."

Those words brought both assurance and solace to Eric as he tramped the maze of streets around the Donegall Road and Sandy Row.

Photographs of his political opponents seemed to leer at him from nearly every lamp-post.

"They shall not prevail against thee," said God.

"Who is this Eric Smyth anyway?" blared the diatribe from the screeching loudspeakers. "He's a nobody. An illiterate. A loner."

"I am with thee, to deliver thee," said God.

As the campaign intensified through April and into May, Eric became more convinced that he could win a seat on the City Council. Some believed that he would be left trailing in Billy Dixon's wake. A non-starter.

Eric believed in God.

Increasingly, too, as he met the electorate on the hustings, he began to believe in himself as well.

But how would it all turn out on the day that mattered? What would the count reveal?

Polling day, 20th May, was a hectic one for Eric. He visited polling stations, talked to his election agents, met and tried to coax some dithering voters ...

When it came to the count, Eric was tired, but confident. Exhausted and expectant.

There was a charged silence as the returning officer stood up to declare the results.

Billy Dixon had been given a substantial vote. Would be re-elected on the first preference vote ...

Then came the one that he had been waiting for ...

"Smyth, Eric. Nine hundred and twenty four."

Tremendous.

It wasn't enough to see him elected on the first preference vote. But it was good. A very promising start.

As the second round of the count began, Eric was nervous. He felt he could make it this time. Or would he?

A senior official who was overseeing the count smiled reassuring at him.

"Mr Smyth, you are going to be elected here," he said simply, and his prediction proved to be true.

Eric Smyth, the no-hoper, the fill-the-gap man, whose love was for the people, and whose faith was in God, was elected as a city councillor for the Donegall Road ward on the Belfast City Council.

How he praised God!

The God who had guided him and strengthened him during the storms of an electoral campaign was now leading him onwards into calmer, but totally uncharted waters.

No doubt there would be difficulties, he was going to be forced into devising his own system of compensating for lack of formal education; just as he had done in Michelin many years before.

Although there would probably be practical problems up ahead so also would there seem to be endless opportunities.

There would be opportunities to meet lots of ordinary, honest, hardworking people. There would be the opportunity to represent those people, the real people of the inner city, on the City Council.

Most important of all to Eric, would be the opportunity to stand for his God, and His principles, when matters of a moral or spiritual nature came up for discussion.

Councillor Eric Smyth had stepped yet another rung up the ladder of God's plan for his life.

# CHAPTER FOURTEEN

# WHAT'S HAPPENING HERE, LORD?

AS HE CONTINUED HIS FULL-TIME WORK FOR THE LORD IN AUGHRIM STREET THERE WERE MANY THINGS FOR WHICH ERIC PRAISED GOD. BUT THERE WERE SETBACKS, DIFFICULTIES AND DISCOURAGEMENTS, AS WELL.

It wasn't all sunshine.

There were mountains and valleys, crests and troughs, ups and downs.

The nature of his work was slow. And repetitive. There were many times when he returned to reinforce and explain messages to what were only mildly interested people. Then they didn't seem to be interested at all any longer.

Told Eric not to bother coming back.

And he just had to begin again. Somewhere else with someone else.

Following his election to the City Council, Eric was chatting one day to Billy Gault, a fellow DUP councillor.

"Eric, I have a wee house in Tiger Bay. It is in Greenmount Street, off North Queen Street. We were wondering if you could make any use of it. To have meetings in. Start some sort of Gospel work, you know?" Billy enquired.

"Give me time to think it over, and pray about it, Billy," Eric replied. "I will let you know soon."

When he had given it some consideration, weighed up the pros and cons, and spent some time in prayer, Eric informed his friend that he would be interested in taking the house in Greenmount Street. To use it as a centre for Gospel outreach in the district.

It would mean extra work. Whilst not wanting to desert Aughrim Street, and his friends and constituents in Sandy Row, he nonetheless felt that God had led Billy Gault to approach him about Greenmount Street.

Perhaps God had further plans for him. Billy's proposal certainly represented an opportunity to work and witness in the Tiger Bay area of North Belfast.

First task, then, was to transform the house into a meeting place. Christians from the locality helped Eric to brush the place out, repair the worst of the falling plasterwork and replace the sad-looking drooping wallpaper, and bring in seating.

When the larger upstairs bedroom had undergone a conversion, it was time for Eric and those who had so willingly pledged to help him, to introduce themselves, and their message, God's message, of the Gospel, to the local residents.

The best way to do this, they agreed, was to arrange a Gospel Mission.

On 18th August, 1981, the mission commenced. Eric and his team went systematically from door-to-door inviting the local people to attend.

Soon they started to come.

A trickle at first. Then a stream.

Eventually a river. The two or three of the first nights, brought more, who in turn, brought more, who in turn ...

Wesley Graham, the evangelist, spoke earnestly.

Eric Smyth and his friends, prayed feverently.

By the middle of the second week thirty people were jammed, crammed into the once-upon-a-time bedroom that now served as a meeting-room. On pleasant August evenings, the atmosphere could only be described as warm, the contact, close!

God moved mightily in those meetings.

Four people came to know Jesus Christ as Saviour. This was an answer to prayer, and a result of sustained spiritual effort.

When the meetings were over, the work wasn't. There remained so much still to be done.

There had been an interest generated in the North Queen Street area. New converts needed instruction. Vital channels to the community had been opened.

Concerned Christians approached Eric.

"You must stay here and continue this work," they urged. "God is in this thing. Start more meetings. Something for the children. A teaching group of some kind. This could be the start of something big. The flock is growing and the lambs need fed."

Having always maintained that preaching wasn't for him, Eric now faced a dilemma. He poured out his heart to God, as he had done so often before.

"Lord, what is happening here?" he asked in anguish. "These people are pushing me to preach and teach. You know that I can't do that. Yes, I can walk plenty, and talk plenty. but to stand up and read the Bible and preach and teach new converts. How could I do that, Lord?"

For weeks he wrestled with it.

To start teaching these new Christians he would have to read the Bible and explain it.

To start a regular Gospel outreach he would have to read the Bible and expound it.

As he contemplated these matters his mind was drawn repeatedly to the potter and the clay.

He just couldn't escape it.

"Can I not do with you as this potter? said the Lord."

The Potter was able.

The Potter was skilful.

But the clay had to be ready. Soft, malleable, just the right consistency. Prepared to be moulded.

He consulted regularly with a number of Christians who had worked with him so tirelessly during the Mission.

"If you take it on Eric," they assured him, "we will be right behind you. We will do everything that we can to support you."

Eventually Eric submitted to what he considered to be the will of God, and to the gentle persuasion of his friends.

The people seemed keen.

The door was lying wide-open.

He was willing to enter. Seize the opportunity.

He would give it a go.

# CHAPTER FIFTEEN

# DOWN, BUT NOT OUT

DURING THE AUTUMN OF 1981 THE HOUSE IN GREENMOUNT STREET BECAME A HIVE OF ACTIVITY.

A community Gospel meeting was started each Tuesday evening.

Then came the prayer meeting and Bible study each Wednesday evening. Eric needn't have worried so much about this. God had help at hand.

Shortly after its commencement, Jackie Butler volunteered to take charge of this meeting, and did so faithfully each week.

The people of the district liked the Tuesday evening meeting and came. The new Christians loved the Wednesday group.

Then Eric and his friends decided that something should be done for the children of Tiger Bay. There seemed to be so many of them about. Every corner you turned there were more. Swinging around lamp-posts, kicking balls idly against walls. Or just standing, sitting or loitering lazily about.

A Sunday School was begun.

Every Sunday afternoon at 3:30 pm up to seventy children packed into the little bedroom. It was bulging at the seams.

Friday night became Children's Meeting night. The local children, many of them different from those who came to Sunday School, flocked to it as well.

God seemed to bless the outreach in all its aspects in that first autumn and winter session. Everybody was so enthusiastic.

Soon it was realised that the single bedroom was far too small. Eric was surrounded by a willing band of helpers and they performed another conversion, knocking down a wall and making two bedrooms into one, giving more space.

Things were progressing.

In Christian work, as in any other activity, however, the first flush of enthusiasm can wane. What was once a one-day-wonder can become an every day routine.

This happened to Eric.

In the second year of his work in Greenmount Street he began to lose the initial fire of zeal for the outreach.

He still arranged the meetings. Methodically but mechanically.

He still visited in the neighbourhood. More from a sense of duty, though, than any burning spiritual desire.

Two things were happening to him. Affecting his Christian commitment. Drawing him away from his one-time fervour.

Firstly, he began to fell alone. Isolated. He wasn't a recognised minister. The folks who helped him were extremely supportive. Eric recognised that. But they weren't full-time at this work. They had other daytime jobs.

Eric was doing this all day, every day, but he had nobody else, in the same situation, to turn to. To share with. He had no soul-mate.

As the number of meetings began to increase, so too did the pressures and responsibilities.

Eric had nobody to whom he could unburden his deepest concerns, except Frances, who did her best. She, however, was struggling to rear their six children with no steady income.

That left Eric thrown totally back upon God. For everything.

God would have been more than able to help and strengthen in far more ways than Eric ever needed. But therein lay Eric's second, and probably more serious, problem.

He was becoming preoccupied with other things. God was being shoved into second place.

Since he felt out-on-a-limb in his Christian work Eric threw himself headlong into his other interest. The busy-ness and new-fangledness of local politics.

When his ministry in the little house in Greenmount Street made him feel isolated, his City Council seat made him feel important. Inflated his ego.

It was here that he began to compromise. He didn't do what he promised himself that he would. He didn't bring God in with him to the City Hall.

God was for Greenmount Street. And Aughrim Street.

It was fine to talk about God there.

But no. Not in the City Hall. God was left at the door of the Council chamber. His Christian faith could prove embarrassing to him in there.

Soon he was mixed-up. Disillusioned. Downhearted.

What was the point in going on?

The initial passion for the work had waned to a surely-not-another-meeting-tonight type of treadmill experience.

By the late summer of 1982 he was contemplating packing the whole thing in. He would give it all up and take a job again. That way, he reckoned, he would make a bit of steady money, meet other people and he could do a bit of visitation on the odd evening when it suited him.

Although disenchanted with what he saw as the monotonous sameness and spiritual loneliness of his once-exciting Christian work, Eric never lost contact with what had now become known as the Martyrs Memorial Free Presbyterian Church on the Ravenhill Road. The leadership there had helped him with the work in Greenmount Street providing minibus transport for the Childrens' meeting.

He attended the Morning Service every Sunday. It was always a thrill to hear Dr. Paisley preach. Since his teenage years that big man, more than any other had been an encouragement to Eric. He deemed the straight-talking politician and preacher a 'true servant of God.'

It was in the Martyrs Memorial Church, one Sunday morning, that something happened which changed the whole course of Eric's Christian service ...

# CHAPTER SIXTEEN

# RAYS OF SUNSHINE, PANGS OF PAIN

---

THE TREE-LINED RAVENHILL ROAD WAS DRESSED IN ITS AUTUMN OUTFIT THAT SUNDAY MORNING.

Eric was one of the first to arrive for the early morning prayer meeting.

He sat quietly, waiting for others appear.

A wet blanket of depression enveloped him. Dampening his spirit. Chilling his soul.

People filed in respectfully, whispering polite pleasantries to each other.

Eric nodded his head to most of them.

Special friends were privileged to catch a glimpse of a faint and fleeting forced smile.

One of those special friends was Sam Lowry.

As he passed behind him, on his way to a seat, Sam tapped Eric on the shoulder. Leaning forward he spoke softly into his ear.

"There's a man from Singapore would like to speak to you, Eric, down in Dr. Paisley's office after this prayer meeting," he said. "He's called Dr. Peter Ng."

"Wants to speak to ME?" Eric was surprised.

He had allowed himself to lapse into a mental state when he believed that the people who really wanted to speak to him were growing fewer by the day.

"Yes. Wants to speak to you." Sam grinned as he spoke. "You had better go down and see him."

When the prayer meeting was over, Eric did just that.

From the minute he met him, Eric liked Pastor Ng.

Small man, broad smile, warm welcome. His face shone.

In addition to everything else about this radiant Christian. Eric was to discover that although he would never be able to pronounce the man's name, he could actually spell it!

Time was short, so it didn't take the pastor from Singapore long to come to the point.

"Dr. Paisley tells me that you have a great little work going here in the city. Visiting amongst the working class people, helping them in their homes, preaching to them, teaching them the Word. Would you like to come in under the banner of the Jesus Saves Mission?"

Eric sat silently for a moment or two.

He looked over to where Dr. Ng sat, waiting his reply. There could be no doubting the sincerity of the approach.

"I would need to know a bit about it before I could commit myself," was Eric's apparently cautious response. Inwardly, he would be delighted to come in under any banner at all that would welcome him, provided that it was spiritually sound.

"That's understandable," Pastor Ng replied.

He then took ten minutes and outlined the history, beliefs, doctrines and future plans of the Jesus Saves Mission to an intent listener.

As he talked, Eric became increasingly interested.

The Jesus Saves Mission, as he explained it, operated on very much the same principles, but obviously on a much larger scale, than the work in Greenmount Street.

When Pastor Ng had finished his comprehensive description, Eric felt that he could open his heart to this patently genuine man.

"Thank you very much for telling me all that, Pastor," he began, "You have no idea how much this invitation means to me. Coming as it does at this time. You see I was considering giving up the work in Greenmount Street. I felt that it wasn't worthwhile struggling on with it. We haven't been seeing as much blessing as we would have liked recently so I was beginning to wonder if God was in it at all ..."

After pausing for breath, and his first real smile of the morning, Eric continued, "But now this suggestion of yours sheds a new light on everything. I would be very keen for us to join the Jesus Saves Mission. I like the sound of it.

But since there are a number of committed believers who help me, I would need to ask their opinion, and seek their approval."

Pastor Ng nodded knowingly.

Again this was understandable.

"Talk to your friends and let me know in your own good time," was how the Pastor left it with Eric.

When he mentioned his conversation with Dr. Ng to his friends in Greenmount Street they were, as he had expected they would be, delighted. They would be only too pleased to be affiliated to the Jesus Saves mission. It would provide them with a much-needed identity.

At least they would be recognised as a church. They would be more than just an odd assortment of Christians holding an odd assortment of meetings. The occupants of an unoccupied house in Tiger Bay.

Eric contacted Dr. Ng and passed on everyone's wholehearted endorsement of his offer.

It wasn't long after that, then, until all the activity in Greenmount Street took on a new meaning. Someone was interested in helping them. And they were keen to respond.

Eric's sense of despondency lifted too.

Now there were others whom he could talk to. He was part of a worldwide team, all united in the same kind of work.

Preaching, teaching, counselling, visiting.

Representatives from the founding church in Singapore made regular visits to Belfast to encourage, help and advise during 1983.

They were pleased with the progress they observed.

And said so.

Eric's fellow workers in Greenmount Street began to work more energetically. With more spiritual zeal and with a more intense concern for the residents of North Belfast.

They undertook the major task of converting the downstairs area of the house into one large meeting room. This project wasn't without its snags, but they managed it.

Four of them, Jackie Butler, George Reid, Billy Neeson and Eric, nicknamed themselves 'The A Team.'

"You name it, we will try it!" was their motto.

Billy Brown, another dedicated helper, was 'the spark'. He re-wired the whole place.

When all the structural alterations were finished, everybody pitched in to help with the redecorating.

They were pleased with their efforts.

When the meetings recommenced after the refurbishment God began to bless again. Numbers started to increase. The enlarged accommodation and genuine welcome they received encouraged people to return time and time again.

Souls were saved.

God was honoured, and He in turn honoured the revitalised effort.

Eric had begun to clamber out of his pit of despair.

Rays of sunshine were beginning to spill out around the edges of his eclipse.

He was visiting with more enthusiasm, preaching with more fervour, praying with more faith ...

Just one thing niggled him though.

It was like a thorn in your thumb that you had forgotten about until you pressed it on something, and then went 'Ouch!'

It was the City Hall. Especially the council chamber.

He enjoyed his work as a city councillor. No question about that. Helped his constituents in every possible way. Was always available to plead their case. Witnessed to them readily about his faith at their doors and by their firesides when the opportunity presented itself.

The thing which really got to him was that he couldn't drag himself to stand up boldly and be counted for God in the often heated debate of the city council chamber.

He was scared.

He felt shackled and muzzled by an unseen but powerful enemy.

Just that one little thing annoyed him.

Everything else had started to sparkle again.

Except that.

It spoiled the sparkle for him often.

He left the council meetings feeling defeated.

Although he had done everything in his power to represent the people of the Donegall Road, he had done absolutely nothing as an ambassador for Christ.

He had let God down.

He remembered a picture he saw once of a man who had two faces which looked in opposite directions.

Eric felt like that.

He had two faces. Two distinct personalities.

A schizophrenic Christian!

What could he do about it?

# CHAPTER SEVENTEEN

# QUALIFICATION, TREPIDATION, ORDINATION

---

IN FEBRUARY 1984 ERIC RECEIVED A TELEGRAM. IT WAS AN INVITATION TO ATTEND THE EASTER CONFERENCE OF THE JESUS SAVES MISSION CHURCH IN SINGAPORE. ALL EXPENSES WOULD BE PAID.

What a fix that put him in!

He wanted to accept the invitation. It would allow him to meet other ministers of the church and learn more about the set up.

But what about Frances? And the family? Six of them. If he went it would leave his wife with the sole responsibility for the children.

When he expressed his concerns to her, though, she encouraged him to go out to Singapore. She appreciated how much his involvement with the Jesus Saves Mission meant to him.

And when he was happy, she was happy.

"You go ahead, Eric. Tell them you will be there. I will manage OK. Somehow. Anyway, it's only for two weeks," she persuaded him.

So Eric accepted the invitation.

Flew out to Singapore.

On arriving there he was escorted to the conference site, on St John's Island.

During the Easter week, each day's activities began at 6.00am with a communal prayer meeting. Then throughout the day there were preaching, teaching and praying sessions. Many of the delegates were fasting. The climax of each day was the evening service which lasted for two hours.

Eric enjoyed the variety of meetings and the warmth of the welcome he received. There were a number of opportunities to tell of the work in Belfast, which in comparison to the scale of the conference seemed very insignificant, and to Eric as he thought of home, very, very far anyway!

Early in the week Eric had been asked if he would address the final conference gathering on the Friday evening, and agreed to do so.

That evening almost four hundred people crammed into the main conference hall. It had been a pleasantly warm day and everyone had come to the last main meeting of the week with eager anticipation. They had been drawn closer to God during the conference and were on a spiritual "high".

When Eric began to speak he felt a very real, almost uncanny, sense that God was with him. Everybody seemed to be hanging on to his words. Many of the congregation were writing busily in little notebooks.

"The fields are white already to harvest," was his chosen text, from John chapter four.

"The fields are white," he challenged his audience. "God has his harvest ready for reaping. In America. In Asia. In Australia. Even in Belfast. Troubles or no troubles. All He needs now are the reapers. Those who will go out and gather it in ..."

It was powerful, passionate preaching. God was in that place, everybody knew it.

When the meeting finished nobody moved.

Nobody wanted to go anywhere else, afraid of moving out of the awesome presence of God.

Many cried out in spiritual anguish.

Dozens rededicated their lives to God and His service.

About an hour later, when the audience started, rather reluctantly, to make towards their accommodation, Pastor Tan, a senior figure in the movement approached Eric.

"That was wonderful, Eric!" he exclaimed. "What a tremendous sense of the power of God. We have decided that we are going to ordain you as a minister of the Jesus Saves Mission church."

Eric was flabbergasted.

"But surely you can't ordain me," he objected. "I have no qualifications at all. None."

During that week of conference Eric had met so many well-educated people that he was embarrassed, almost to the extent of becoming neurotic, about his lack of formal education.

Pastor Tan seemed unimpressed by his protests.

"A lot depends on what you count as qualifications," he went on to explain. "We know how things have developed back in Belfast. God is blessing your work. For us that is qualification enough. We feel that it would be wrong to stand in the way of the Lord."

He paused momentarily to allow Eric to consider this, before continuing, to explain the procedure for the ordination.

"We know that you can't write very well, so instead of asking you to sit a written paper or anything like that, we would like you to come before the inner council of the Jesus Saves Movement tomorrow," he said.

"What does that mean?" Eric enquired. He had a vision of about forty learned men staring at him from under their eyebrows and over their glasses.

Pastor Tan laughed, sensing Eric's trepidation.

"We only want to have a friendly chat with you," he replied. "Perhaps you could answer one or two simple questions for us."

On the Saturday afternoon, Eric met the inner council of the Jesus Saves Mission.

There were fifteen of them. Not forty!

It was, as Pastor Tan had promised, a more relaxed affair than Eric had envisaged. They asked him questions, and when he had answered their questions, he was given the opportunity to ask questions of his own.

Which he did.

After an hour of cordial exchange on the work of God around the world, including such locations as Aughrim Street and Greenmount Street, Eric was asked to wait outside for a short period.

When invited to return to the room he was informed that he had been unanimously accepted as a minister of their church and would be ordained at the evening service on the next day, Sunday.

His inferiority complex regarding his lack of academic prowess must have surfaced in the interview, for the council members thought it necessary to reassure him.

"Don't worry about your lack of qualifications," they said. "It is obvious to us that you have a definite calling of God to do Christian work. God has been blessing your service for Him in Belfast. Evidence of the power and presence of God in any spiritual work means more to us than paper qualifications. College is important, but not essential. There are unique situations in which our God performs miracles."

The ordination service was a pack-out. Again a very real sense of God pervaded the place. At the simple, scriptural ceremony, Eric Smyth was ordained a minister of the Jesus Saves Mission church.

The next two days were spent meeting other ministers, discussing the possibilities of developing the work in Belfast and phoning home to Frances.

On Wednesday he flew back to Northern Ireland.

To Frances and the family.

To Greenmount Street and Aughrim Street.

To Sandy Row, The Donegall Road and the City Hall.

He felt pleased to be recognised as a servant of God but slightly apprehensive as to how he would be accepted with another title.

Councillor Eric Smyth had now become Councillor Rev Eric Smyth.

He wasn't long home until the newly ordained minister had arranged for the official opening of the house in Greenmount Street as a Jesus Saves Mission church.

The event was widely publicised and took place in May, 1984. Eric's old friend and patient spiritual mentor, Dr Paisley, performed the opening ceremony, and gave a challenging address.

Christians from other churches plus residents from the neighbourhood squeezed into the little house-church.

The downstairs was packed, the upstairs was packed, the non-seated spilled out on to the street ...

The Jesus Saves Mission Church had arrived in Belfast.

# CHAPTER EIGHTEEN

# GIVE A CHILD A HOME

NOEL AND MARIE STEVENSON, LIFE-LONG FRIENDS OF ERIC AND FRANCES, HAD STARTED TO FOSTER CHILDREN.

The Smyths were intrigued by the succession of babies and young children that passed through the Stevenson home.

One night, on returning from a visit to their friends' home, Eric was very thoughtful.

Frances noticed it.

"What's wrong Eric?" she enquired after some time. "You are very quiet."

"I was just wondering if we couldn't give a child a home" he replied, pleased to be granted the opportunity to share his thoughts.

"Funny you should say that," his wife sounded excited almost, as she responded to his suggestion. "I have been wondering about that myself. In fact I have to confess that it has crossed my mind many a time. Then again, I think that when we are giving six of them a home we are doing rightly!"

"You know that's not what I mean," Eric went on. "I mean fostering a child the way Noel and Marie do."

"I know exactly what you mean, love," Frances consoled him. "It would be great to give a needy child a home. I'm sure our children would love another baby about the house. I will make some enquiries about it. Noel and Marie could help us I'm sure."

When she had spoken to their friends about their interest in fostering, Eric and she were encouraged to make approaches to various agencies who arranged foster parents.

Some of their initial enquiries proved fruitless. For one reason or another, nothing came of them. It seemed, as the days passed, that their chances of ever becoming foster parents were receding.

Then Frances spotted the advertisement in the newspaper.

FOSTER PARENTS REQUIRED

Apply to: North and West Social Services, Cupar Street, Belfast.

Just what they had been looking for!

When she had discussed it with Eric, Frances did as the advert instructed.

She applied to the North and West Social Services. To have Eric and she registered as foster parents.

First signs were hopeful.

Nobody said "No!"

And because nobody had as yet said "No", Frances began to expect a social worker to arrive on their doorstep one day with a baby in her arms and say, like Pharaoh's daughter in the Bible "Here, take this baby and mind him for me, and I will pay you for it!"

She was to learn that it didn't work like that.

Frances began to realise that the people from the social services had to be extremely prudent as to where they placed their babies. Not just any household would do.

All the members of the family would have to be carefully screened.

Hence the interviews.

First with Eric and Frances together, as a couple.

Then with Eric and Frances separately, as individuals.

And what about the family? The six young Smyths, the resident children.

How would they respond to the sudden arrival of a newcomer in their home? A baby perhaps, or a toddler.

Interested? Protective? Unaffected? Jealous?

Their opinions were sought and anticipated reactions analysed.

After all the forms had been completed and all the interviews had been conducted, then the waiting began.

They waited for news. And waited, and waited for news.

It was agonising.

Would they be accepted? Approved? Or not?

When the answer came it proved to have been worth waiting for.

Eric and Frances were informed that they had been approved as foster parents, and that they should prepare to receive their first foster-child.

They were thrilled to bits!

Peter came into the Smyth household on October 2nd, 1984.

He was four days old.

What excitement his arrival generated!

What a mixed reaction his day-by-day development evoked!

Eric and Frances cared for him attentively. They were experienced and confident.

Karen, aged seventeen, wanted to nurse him at every available opportunity.

The middle-order boys liked him a lot, but only talked about him a little. It wasn't macho for teenage males to appear even remotely interested in babies.

Andrew, aged five, had no inhibitions. He was fascinated by the crying, sleeping, bottle-sucking bundle of humanity.

Everybody loved him.

Christmas was always a special time for the Smyth family.

It was an extra-special time that year.

The whole family were learning a lesson in caring.

After the joy and hearth-and-home-happiness of Christmas, came January, 1985.

Long, grey, chilly January.

And with January came the news that Peter was to be relocated into a permanent home.

He would be collected from his foster parents on January 4th.

What a day that was!

They had all become so attached to Peter.

What gloom his departure generated.

Eric made sure that he was out of the house on church and council business all day. He couldn't bear to see the little one go. Couldn't face it at all.

He said his goodbyes before he went out.

The family were all glad, for once, that school had recommenced after the holiday. At least they wouldn't be around when "wee Peter" as they all called him, disappeared.

They said their goodbyes before they went out.

That left only Frances.

Mother.

Loving mother. Caring mother. Foster mother.

She opened the door bravely when the two social workers arrived. She watched tearfully as they loaded some baby-type things into the car.

When the final moment came and one of the social workers was carrying Peter out of the house, Frances left the house too.

She followed them out.

Then crossed the street.

From the doorway of a neighbour-woman's house, with a neighbour-woman's comforting arm around her shoulder, Frances wept silently as she watched Peter, who had been her "son" for three months, being driven away.

To a new, and permanent, home.

The whole family were learning another lesson.

A lesson in sharing.

A new chapter had begun in the life of the irrepressible Smyths.

Frances, who had experienced, and so far survived all the joys and trials of a natural mother, had just been introduced to the joys and trials of a foster mother.

And Councillor Rev Eric Smyth had added a new string to his bow.

A new title to his collection.

Foster father.

# CHAPTER NINETEEN

# DEMOLITION JOB

---

BIG DECISIONS HAD TO BE MADE IN 1985.

The first was concerning the work in Aughrim Street, on Sandy Row. Following upon the upsurge in the interest in the Jesus Saves Mission in the north end of the city, Eric realised that he would not have either the physical or spiritual stamina to continue overseeing the work in Aughrim Street as well.

He had been trying to divide himself for the previous four years.

Found it hard.

So reluctantly he decided to give it up.

He would hand it over to others who were well prepared to continue the outreach there.

A second and very important decision had to be made with regard to his future involvement in local politics. As councillor for Donegall Road and Sandy Row.

1985 was election year again.

A number of his fellow DUP councillors expected him to stand for re-election. Just took it for granted that he would.

They were surprised, then, when Eric made known that he was contemplating standing down.

"Why would you do a thing like that, Eric?" they enquired sincerely. "You have worked well for the ward and the people like you. You should have no trouble at all in retaining your seat."

Dr Paisley rang him.

"We must meet and talk about this election, Eric," he suggested.

Eric agreed that they should meet.

Thursday morning at ten-thirty was arranged.

Events, however, took an unexpected turn.

Eric did not sleep a wink on Wednesday night.

Not from anxiety about his future in the City Hall, though, but from a much more acute and pressing problem.

Toothache!

The severe excruciating pain of a rotten tooth!

He was up and he was down.

He drank hot water. Then cold water.

He just ate tablets. Chewed them up like Smarties.

Still the pain didn't go away.

And when it came ten-thirty on Thursday morning, Eric wasn't with Dr Paisley.

We was in the dentist's having a tooth out!

Dr Paisley couldn't wait. He had other appointments.

So the meeting didn't take place.

And Eric wasn't persuaded to stand for re-election.

He was determined that he wouldn't. That he shouldn't.

He had his own reasons for standing down as a councillor. Although pleased at the confidence which his colleagues appeared to place in him Eric knew that he had let God, and himself down in the City Hall. And he wanted to be out of it.

Anyway, he had other things on which he had decided to concentrate.

To him these were more significant things, because of the eternal nature of the expected outcome.

Eric wanted to devote all his time, all his energies, and all his spiritual zeal, to the rapidly developing outreach in Greenmount Street.

The Jesus Saves Mission.

It was in early October 1985 that he finally handed over the work in Aughrim Street to his friends there. Said his sad goodbyes.

To concentrate wholly on the new venture.

Now that he had only the one church to care for, Eric relished the challenge of forging ahead on every front.

Seeing things done. Better. Faster.

And with loads and loads of blessing.

Then came the big shock!

Satan was ready to take a lot of the steam out of him! And his keen-type Christian aides!

Towards the end of that very same month, October 1985, they learnt with horror that their house-church was scheduled for demolition.

Greenmount Street was coming down.

Every brick of it. The bulldozers would soon be moving in.

The entire area had been earmarked for redevelopment. All in the cause of a brighter, better, buzzing Belfast.

When they first heard this news, Eric and his team were bewildered.

What would they do?

What a thing to happen. Just when the work had revived, souls were being saved, and Eric had freed himself from all other commitments to allow himself to go full blast at it ...

# CHAPTER TWENTY

# PLANNING, PRAYING, PAYING

---

AS THEY AGONISED OVER THE FLATTENING OF GREEN-MOUNT STREET, THE CONGREGATION OF THE JESUS SAVES MISSION CAME TO REALISE THAT THEY HAD ONE POWER-FUL ALLY. THE ONE WHO HAD LED THEM TO COMMENCE THE OUTREACH IN TIGER BAY WASN'T GOING TO DESERT THEM NOW.

God was on their side.

Panic gave way to prayer.

Consternation to consultation.

They applied to the Housing Executive for alternative accommodation or ground on which to erect a new church building.

When the reply came from the Housing Executive it wasn't terribly encouraging.

It said in effect, "Sorry. Never heard of you. The Jesus Saves Mission is not a recognised church."

This was merely a set-back. Certainly not a defeat.

God was still on their side.

Eric and his friends diligently pursued their application and a public enquiry was set up to examine the issue.

After much patient explanation in the City Planning Office, and much earnest prayer in Greenmount Street, the public enquiry ruled in favour of the Jesus Saves Mission.

They were offered an alternative location at a reasonable price.

It was a plumb site.

Situated at the junction of Limestone Road and North Queen Street it would be easily accessible to a wide area of North Belfast. Ideal. Couldn't have been better.

The agreed price was four thousand pounds.

God was still on their side.

And was prepared to prove it.

He had opened up an irresistible opportunity to the Jesus Saves Mission to establish itself as a spiritual force in the district.

To procure a site and erect a suitable church building.

But what about the financial aspect of the matter?

They were a small company. Rich in love and faith, but not so liberally endowed with ready cash.

Four thousand pounds to them was a mountain of money. And that was only for the site!

How could they ever hope to raise enough money to buy the site and then build a church?

The answer was simple.

Faith.

They had faith in their God.

Eric adopted as his motto in those stepping-out, going-ahead days, a text from Hebrews chapter eleven.

"Without faith it is impossible to please God."

They all wanted to please God in their church. In their neighbourhood. In their lives.

So they needed faith.

Their trust in God was rewarded.

First came a gift of four thousand pounds from Singapore. Payment for the site.

They were off to a flying start!

Then came the planning, the praying, the paying, the praying.

More paying. Then more praying.

The "A" Team now had another job to tackle.

"You name it. We will try it."

This time it was raising funds.

A site was all right, but it would be cold at night.

They needed a building on it.

Bricks and bricklayers, pipes and plumbers, paint and painters were all going to cost money.

The Christians of the church worked hard and donated liberally.

Soon they had raised fifteen thousand pounds. This represented sacrificial giving in many cases.

Within a year of acquiring the site they had started to build.

And God was still on their side.

As money was needed, money was provided.

A generous and deeply committed Christian from Singapore forwarded the remainder of the sum required to erect the church, as an interest free loan.

As the building began to rise out of the mud and rubble of that corner site the friendship and fellowship of the church members increased.

The excitement and anticipation grew!

They were seeing a dream fulfilled. A goal achieved.

A permanent base for the Jesus Saves Mission would soon be established in North Belfast.

When the brick work was up, the roof went on. Then in went the ceiling, the floor, the windows, the heating ...

Next it was plastered, painted and polished.

Soon it would be ready. Finished. Fit for occupation.

Eric and his loyal congregation appeared publicly and collectively delighted whilst inwardly and individually they were somewhat daunted at the prospect. What a chance to witness in the district! What a challenge to them all!

# CHAPTER TWENTY-ONE

# OPENING UP, AGAIN

WHEN THE NEW BUILDING WAS COMPLETED EARLY IN 1987 ERIC HAD ANOTHER OPENING CEREMONY TO ARRANGE.

In many ways it would be different from that first official opening of the Jesus Saves Mission in Greenmount Street three years previously.

It was a brand new and purpose-built church that they were opening. Not a renovated house-cum-church.

It stood proudly on its own, if still rather cluttered, site. It wasn't a house amongst identical houses, in a street amongst identical streets.

It could hold at least ten times as many people as the house in Greenmount Street.

Yet some elements about the opening of the larger, brighter more modern church would be exactly the same as before.

For one, it was the same faithful God who had led them to open in their humble first base who had now brought them thus far.

God, the Almighty, the all-loving, all-caring, all-provident, was and is an eternal constant.

Secondly, it was the same nucleus of devoted Christians who had worked for funds and prayed in faith to make this new building possible.

It was the same man, too, who was invited to perform both opening ceremonies. Who else but Eric's close friend and trusted spiritual guide, Dr. Ian Paisley.

The towering mass of the Cavehill, hazy in the afternoon sunshine, provided the backdrop, and the roar of the passing city traffic provided the background music, as Dr. Paisley turned the key in the front door of the simple building.

He declared it open, "in the name of the Father, the Son and the Holy Spirit."

On entering the foyer he was asked to unveil a small plaque with the inscription:-

### JESUS SAVES MISSION CHURCH
*This church was dedicated to the glory of God*
*on Saturday 23rd May, 1987*
*by*
*Rev. Dr. Ian R. K. Paisley MP, MEP*
*Blessed are they that dwell in thy house:*
*they will be still praising thee. Psalm 84 v. 5*

People were packed in everywhere. Friends, neighbours, Christians from other local churches ... they were all there, crushed into every available centimetre of seating space.

Those who couldn't find a seat in the main hall were accommodated in the anteroom. Some just had to stand in the entrance hall or round the walls of the little room at the back.

Those who came late were faced with a cruel choice. Either stand outside or go home. The building couldn't hold another person!

It was very warm.

Many people dressed in their Sunday best that Saturday afternoon were sweltered.

Eric welcomed the congregation and gave a short history of the work of the Jesus Saves Mission in north Belfast.

Nelson McCausland played the piano accordion and sang.

Dr. Paisley gave the address. He spoke with power and yet with tenderness.

It was all about doors. Open doors, closed doors ...

Jesus said, "I am the door: by me if any man enter in, he shall be saved ..."

Despite the superheated, overcrowded conditions the audience listened intently.

When, at the end, Dr. Paisley challenged those who were "still outside of the door to heaven," to "get the matter settled today," the response was tremendous.

Nine people came forward for counselling.

Question.

Where do you put nine people seeking peace in their souls, and their counsellors, when the building is jam-packed and you are trying to serve tea to everybody?

Answer.

Simple. You kindly ask all the pins-and-needles-riddled-people in the back room to move outside. They will probably be glad of a breath of fresh air anyway!

It worked a treat! A picnic-of-sorts was held in the hitherto 'unlandscaped' grounds. It was fun to improvise. Old oil drums, builders' planks and discarded oddly shaped breeze-blocks were pressed into service. They doubled as seats and tables of highly functional design.

And meanwhile back in the anteroom nine souls had been saved.

What an outpouring of blessing!

The excitement and rejoicing amongst the Christians stretched on well into the evening. And then well into the next day, the Sunday, too ...

It seemed that God had seen fit to stamp the whole venture with His seal of approval.

The Jesus Saves Mission Church had arrived in north Belfast.

In a purpose-built permanent building.

To stay.

# CHAPTER TWENTY-TWO

# LITTLE JOHN

---

THAT BRIGHT MAY DAY, WHEN THE JESUS SAVES MISSION WAS OFFICIALLY OPENED, WAS A FAMILY DAY OUT FOR THE SMYTHS.

Eric, father, was very much in evidence up at the front. The chief controller.

Frances was there, on crutches, having fallen a few days earlier. She was disappointed that she was unable to help with the catering as she would have liked, but walloping crutches would not be welcome in a cramped and steamy kitchen.

There was plenty for her to do, nonetheless. She had to keep a maternal eye on the children.

All six of them were present, and their main occupation was to take turns at looking after the little one whom they had unanimously come to accept as number seven.

John.

Eric and Frances had been asked to foster baby John, and he came into their home on 29th August, 1986, when he was exactly one week old.

From that day, he instantly became part of the family, just as Peter had done before him.

Karen loved to nurse and bath him.

As he grew the boys played with him, on the floor, in his play pen. They nicknamed him, "Our wee monkey," for he seemed to want to climb up on to and out over everything, hanging onto and often half-off the playpen rails, the furniture, anything.

When a couple of the boys were given boxing gloves for Christmas presents in 1987 little John was walking about on steady sturdy legs. They used to challenge him to "toy fights" prodding him gently with the bright red gloves.

How John loved it! He pretended to box back, much to the boys' delight!

And he giggled and giggled and giggled.

Eric loved the affectionate toddler, too.

His chief delight was to plonk John between two of the bigger boys in the front seat of the minibus on the way to collect children for the Sunday School and Childrens' Meeting, and listen to his excited chortling as other boys and girls spoke to him and laughed with him.

Although everyone had always known that John wouldn't be with them forever, it was a fact which they all relegated to the backs of their minds as the days went by. He was so much at home with them. So much a part of everything.

It came as a sudden shock, then, when Eric and Frances were informed by Social Services that John had been allocated to a permanent home.

He would be collected by his new parents on Monday, 7th March, 1988.

The whole family were heartbroken.

Karen had just become engaged to be married and had arranged to have some photographs taken.

She summarised the sense of gloom which hung heavily over the family when she asked Frances one day, "How am I ever going to look happy for a photograph, Mummy?"

On that fateful Monday morning, Karen and the boys all said their fond farewells to John and left.

Some to work. Some to school.

All glad to be out.

Frances had to take John for a final medical examination.

It was hard.

She was acutely conscious of the fact that everything she did for him, she was doing for the last time.

After lunch, Eric, who had decided to remain at home to see John go, was sitting gazing absent-mindedly out of the living room window.

Staring into space. Looking, but not seeing.

Thinking about everything.

Deciding about nothing.

When a car drew into the court car park he was jolted back into reality.

"Frances, here are these people," he called. Then almost as though he had to force himself to say it, "for John."

The toddler in question had just rejoined him in the living room, having come down from his last midday nap with the Smyths.

When the new parents came in, John ran straight to Eric, who had gone to welcome-as-best-he-could the visitors, and clung tightly around his legs.

It was as though he knew that something threatening was about to happen. And he was only eighteen months old.

He sensed the unease. The emotional anguish.

Frances was by now in tears.

Eric couldn't hold back either. He cried too.

The new parents were so understanding. So thoughtful. They gave Frances a box of chocolates.

She, in turn, handed them a letter, all about John, which she had composed carefully and prayerfully the night before.

In the envelope she had included a newspaper cutting which summed up her aim in fostering children. And her hopes for John with his new parents. It said this:

"No child asks to be born. But once he is, he is unquestionably a member of society. Tomorrow he has a role to play. Today, he must be cherished, nurtured and groomed to take up that role successfully."

In the midst of all the silent sobbing and sentimental exchanges, the social worker had a job to do. She carried all of John's clothes and toys out to the car.

Then after much kissing and hugging and crying, they left.

The social worker. The new parents.

And John.

As the car reversed out of the car park, Eric ran up the stairs. And shouted to nobody in particular. To everybody, anybody, who could or couldn't hear "That's it!" he was bawling. "No more! We can't go through all this again!"

When he came downstairs again in fifteen minutes, having regained his composure, Frances knew what was coming.

"I don't think we should take any more children on, love," her husband announced with an air of finality, as he joined her, weeping as she worked at the kitchen sink.

"Sure we still have wee Claire here," Frances reminded him.

Claire was a little girl they had been asked to foster for a short term, pre-adoption.

"Yes, I know that," Eric replied. "But I mean these ones that we keep for years at a time. It's going to kill the whole lot of us to have to give them all up again."

Frances tried to console him. And did, eventually, with the help of the social worker, who had returned to check on them about an hour later. She had been so concerned to see them both so upset that she felt she must call back to make sure that they were both OK.

In the next few weeks Frances kept up a brave face. Had to, for Eric's sake. She didn't dare let him know how she felt, but her heart was breaking too.

There was an appalling emptiness in her mother nature that she must conceal.

The only respite from the anguish she could afford herself was obtained from watching a video, when no one else was around.

It was of John, just before he left. Blond hair and bright blue eyes. Laughing, playing, rolling, running with Eric and the others.

She cried her way through it often.

That yielded a sense of relief. It was a safety valve.

She consoled herself, too, that he had gone to a loving, caring home. To become part of another loving, caring family.

Claire left again in April.

Others came over the summer period.

Some for a week or two. Some for a month or two.

Eric was very busy with his ministry in the Jesus Saves Mission, and chose to forget his resolve of 7th March.

Time, the healer, was closing the wound, left by the parting from John.

Then, on 5th October 1988, Donika arrived with them, aged five months.

Her arrival was to open a whole new chapter in their lives.

Another story entirely.

# CHAPTER TWENTY-THREE

# AN OPEN DOOR

DURING THE LATTER MONTHS OF 1987 AND INTO EARLY 1988 THE WORK IN THE JESUS SAVES MISSION DEVELOPED. NUMBERS IN THE SUNDAY SCHOOL AND AT THE GOSPEL MEETING ON A TUESDAY EVENING INCREASED.

God was blessing the work. Eric was pleased about that.

He felt convinced, as the days went by, however, that he should return to local politics in some capacity. Although he didn't know how, or when, he resolved that if he was ever re-elected, he would have learned from his earlier mistakes. He would stand up for God, and against what he considered to be the rapid decline in social and moral values.

In the summertime of 1988, after little John had gone, and before Donika came, Eric felt that the ought to be doing yet more for God. And the City Hall would afford him the opportunity.

So he laid the matter before the Lord in prayer. Consistently. Frequently.

"Lord, if You want me to go back into the City Council, please show me Your will. I won't be asking anybody round here about it. You will have to open the way for me ..."

God answered his prayer. Doing just that. Showing him. Opening the way.

Two of his former fellow councillors approached him one day, late in 1988.

"Eric, we were wondering if you wouldn't consider standing for re-election to the City Council next May?" they enquired. "Ted Ashby is talking about retiring from politics and standing down from Court Ward, on the Shankill Road. You are well known up there. Would you think about it?"

"Yes, I will. I will think about it," Eric assured them. It was an answer to prayer, no doubt, but he wanted to discuss it with Ted Ashby. He didn't want to tramp on any political toes.

Everything would have to be done fair and square.

Ted and Eric talked the matter over on a number of occasions. Ted found it hard to make up his mind. Some days he thought that he wanted to retire. On other days he didn't. Eric understood his dilemma.

"We will both stand as candidates in Court Ward, Ted," Eric proposed to the older man one day. "There is probably room for both of us in the ward. And if there isn't, I believe that God will show us His way. Let us both stand together."

So it was decided.

The DUP were to have two candidates on the ballot paper, in Court Ward.

Through the earlier making-up-his-mind again days, the I-don't-want-to-make-a-mistake-again days, a verse from the Bible kept repeating itself in Eric's mind.

It was still there in the busy canvassing-on-the-Shankill days.

It was Revelation chapter three verse eight.

"I have set before thee an open door, and no man can shut it."

As he walked up, down and around the Shankill Road he talked to the people about their fears and concerns, their hopes and aspirations.

The troubles were continuing apace.

People were being shot, maimed, killed.

There was edginess. Unease.

Eric told his would-be-constituents what he hoped to do for them in the City Council. As opportunity presented itself he also let them know what the Lord Jesus Christ could do for them in their lives.

In this he sounded convincing.

He spoke from experience.

The people admired his simple sincerity.

But would it be enough to see him elected?

Wednesday, 17th May, was polling day.

The tension mounted, excitement grew to fever pitch.

Eric toured the polling stations and spoke to dithering voters. Same as 1981.

As it came to the close of poll a huge question mark hovered over the result.

Would Ted and he both be elected? They hoped so.

Or only one? Would Ted get back?

"I have set before thee an open door..."

The words had been ringing in Eric's ears all day, but would he get in?

During the count the would-be councillors all flitted nervously about.

Giving each other blank stares or tense tight-lipped smiles depending on the mutual acceptability of their political dogmas.

Then came the returning officer. And the result.

The election was by proportional representation and the quota for election was set at 1400 votes.

On the first count Smyth, Hugh, PUP was elected.

Smyth, Eric had been accorded 1006 votes.

Not enough to see him elected, but a sizeable step along the way.

Ted Ashby didn't get as many unfortunately.

Then the laborious, nerve-jangling procedure of election and elimination began.

Count. After count. After count.

On the sixth count, Ted was eliminated.

Eric was elected on his transferred votes.

Sad for Ted. A challenge for Eric.

God had been pleased to afford him another chance.

Grant him a second opportunity.

To stand up and be counted for Him, in the very same situation where he had once fallen flat on his spiritual mouth and nose.

The council chamber in the City Hall.

Would he be up to it this time?

# CHAPTER TWENTY-FOUR

# DONIKA, ADOPTED AND PROTECTED

---

IN EARLY OCTOBER 1988 FRANCES HAD BEEN ASKED BY LISBURN SOCIAL SERVICES IF SHE AND ERIC WOULD CON-SIDER FOSTERING A FOUR-MONTH OLD GIRL.

They agreed, and on 5th October, Donika arrived with them.

As she began to handle the child from that very first day, some kind of maternal instinct alerted Frances to the fact that there was something different about this little one. She wasn't the same as her own had been, or indeed any of the others which she had fostered.

Donika sat with her legs bent up all the time. She was very tight and stiff. Never floppy or relaxed.

She had a funny way of crying, too. More like a scream than a cry.

Donika, it seemed, was going to need very special attention.

Another initial problem with this little girl was that she couldn't suck a bottle. She had to be spoon-fed with special powdered meals. When she was being fed her arms flailed about incessantly. Spoons and powdered dinners flew.

Frances, and her mother, who helped her in those early-Donika-days, soon discovered the secret of feeding the child. It was to hold both of her hands gently but firmly with one adult hand, and spoon the stuff into her mouth with the other.

It worked!

Eric, Frances and the rest of the family became especially interested in this little girl with physical and mental difficulties.

It was a challenge to care for her. A challenge to which all of them were to prove themselves equal.

After much prayerful consideration Eric and Frances decided to ask the social services if they would be permitted to adopt Donika.

A meeting was held in their home in April 1989 at which they formally requested adoption.

As with the fostering, so with the adoption.

Their request was followed by yet further assessment of the family.

A senior social worker made a number of visits to them during the summer. Talking to them all, observing their consideration in their handling of Donika. The rapport that the family had established with the growing child.

At four o'clock one September afternoon, the senior social worker arrived unexpectedly at the Smyth's home.

This was unusual. But the news was good.

She had come to tell the caring couple that they had been passed as adoptive parents, and advised them to apply to the court for legal adoption of little Donika.

Frances could hardly wait until Eric came home, to tell him.

He was overjoyed.

On the very next morning the pair of them went to court and applied to adopt the little handicapped girl who had so won their hearts.

There was a lot of work with her. But they enjoyed it.

They were fully aware that if they were permitted to adopt her the work would be on-going. But they were prepared for that.

When Donika was ten months old a senior physiotherapist came out to assess her.

She showed Frances how to exercise the stiffened feet and legs in the bath. Then the little one had to be taught how to roll over on the floor. And how to sit up.

A speech therapist came to visit her when she was a year old. She showed Donika pictures of everyday objects, and taught her how to make the signs.

Mark, now in his early twenties, would help his mum and dad out, by looking after Donika for long periods, usually by day.

Eric took his turn at amusing Donika too. Unfortunately for him, though, his turn usually came in the middle of the night!

Singing, "Running over, running over, My cup's full and running over ..." was very pleasant with spinning arms and seventy smiling children at three o'clock on a Sunday afternoon.

It wasn't such fun, however, with spinning arms and one child who couldn't get enough of it, keeping you sitting up, starving, in bed at three o'clock on a Thursday morning!

On 25th April, 1990 Eric and Frances went to court for the adoption case to be heard. Donika was with them. Very much part of the family by now. They loved her so much.

The judge asked them a number of questions about her. Her care. Her handicaps. How had they managed to surmount the additional difficulties which her physical and mental problems had brought with them?

He seemed satisfied.

"You will hear the result of your application in due course," he said at length. "Donika's father must be made aware of your application, you understand. That shouldn't take too long."

It didn't either. Though the month of waiting seemed like a year to Eric and Frances.

On 25th May they were delighted to receive the official adoption papers from the Office of Care and Protection.

The child's name on the documents was Donika Margaret Louise Smyth.

She was theirs. By law. For the rest of her life.

Through all the busy family and legal matters surrounding the adoption of Donika, Eric had been working away down the two main channels of his life.

City councillor of Court Ward.

Minister of the Jesus Saves Mission Church.

As councillor for the area, he opened an office and advice centre in his house.

Many people came.

They came to ask his advice on housing, on benefits, on street lighting ...

They came to ask what he could do about vandalism in the area. Wrecking and smashing and annoying the residents.

The bush telegraph on the Shankill Road spread the word. Eric Smyth really cares.

His Christian work was occupying a lot of his time too.

Norman Patterson, a friend from Malvern Street Pentecostal Church, asked Eric if he would take over the work of organising Christian witness parades on significant days and at a variety of venues across the Province.

Eric prayed about it. Then accepted responsibility for it.

Marching with hundreds of other Christians, displaying posters and distributing Christian literature was to him a wonderful opportunity to witness for Christ.

To show people where he stood, and to tell them about his Saviour.

The Sunday School work in the Jesus Saves mission was growing rapidly. They were soon going to need more accommodation.

When a piece of ground, adjacent to the Church on the Limestone Road, became available for sale, Eric prayed.

It seemed a peculiar prayer. It was a 'laying out of the fleece.'

"Lord, if it is Your will for us to buy this ground for the Sunday School work, please give me one thousand pounds into my hand. Then I will know it's from You."

Seemed a tall order.

Thus he prayed, and left it with the Lord.

Told absolutely no one.

A few months later, when visiting amongst his congregation, an old-age pensioner startled him with a proposal.

"I have a thousand pounds here, Eric, that I have saved up," she said, "I would like you to take it for the use of the Church."

Eric thanked her profusely. And told her of his prayer.

Eric then thanked God profusely, as well. For teaching him another lesson. God works in wondrous ways, and through the most unexpected people.

He had granted Eric his answer. One thousand pounds, into his hand. Exactly as he had requested. But it came, not from some wealthy businessman who could easily afford it, but from an old-age pensioner for whom it meant a soul-searching sacrifice.

Work in the church was encouraging.

Local people were attending the services.

Sunday morning, Sunday evening, Tuesday evening.

It was during an evening service, one winter Sunday, that the Smyth family had a nasty shock.

Eric was on the platform.

Frances and the younger children, including Donika, were there also.

At 7:30 pm, just after Eric had begun his address, the door knocked. Loudly. Urgently. Insistently.

An elder went to the door. Followed by another, for safety.

It was Mark.

"Can you get a message up to my Dad?" he asked, breathlessly. "There has been a bomb at the North Howard Street Army Base and our house is wrecked. The front door is off and the windows are blown in, and ..."

Eric sensed the commotion and stopped speaking.

One of the elders came up, explained the position to him and offered to take charge of the remainder of the service.

The Smyth family left the church and hurried home.

To say the house was "wrecked" was probably overstating it, but it really was in some mess.

The front door was hanging off at a crazy angle.

The windows which weren't of leaded glass were all blown in. The leaded panes hung in all sorts of weird shapes. All humps and hollows.

As they walked through the shattered house, Frances was the first to enter Donika's bedroom.

"Oh, Eric, come quickly and look at this!" she exclaimed.

Eric came quickly. And looked.

Donika's cot, which had been close to the window, was full of splinters of jagged glass. The cover was ripped in places.

On any other night of the week, at that time, Donika would have been in her cot. The thought crossed both of their minds simultaneously.

"If she had been in that cot she would have been scarred for life. May be killed," Eric whispered.

Frances wiped away a tear. Both parents praised God for His preserving care over their family.

Donika was still theirs.

By grace this time.

For the rest of her life.

# CHAPTER TWENTY-FIVE

# MATTHEW

FRANCES AND HER MOTHER WERE PREPARING TO SET OFF
FOR AN EASTER BREAK. IT WAS GOOD FRIDAY 1991.

Amidst the flurry of preparation and organisation, the phone rang.

"Mrs. Smyth, this is your social worker. There is a baby soon to
be born in the Royal. We know there is going to be something wrong
with it. We were wondering if you would consider fostering it?"

Frances replied that she would certainly consider it, but that she
was setting off for a holiday over Easter.

Less than an hour later the phone rang again. Same social worker.

"Remember the baby I was telling you about, Mrs. Smyth?" she
began. "Well, it has been born and it's a boy. He has a number of problems as we expected and is being moved to the Royal Belfast Hospital
for Sick Children. Go off for your break, think it over, and give us a call
when you get back."

The two women went off on holiday. Frances phoned Eric often
and they talked about the baby.

What kind of problems would he have?

Could they manage another child?

They decided that they would certainly try.

Frances could hardly wait to get home.

When the house was more or less back to rights she phoned the social worker.

"Eric and I would like to take on that baby you were telling me about," she volunteered almost straight away.

There was the caution of wisdom in the social worker's reply.

"Do you not think you ought to see him first?" she asked.

Frances agreed. It was wise counsel.

When she did see him the next day in the hospital, the prospective foster-mother fell in love with him at once.

He looked a pathetic little soul. Lying on his tummy, for he couldn't lie on his back. Because of the lesion.

The lesion was a lump, bigger than the baby's head, right in the middle of his back. It was covered by a dressing.

His legs lay limp and loose. Reminded Frances of a cloth doll she used to have as a child. Legs that flopped about all over the place.

Matthew, as the baby had been called, had spina bifida.

Frances sat and looked at him.

She gazed, and gazed and gazed at him.

"How do you work with a baby like that?" was the very practical question she kept asking herself.

A nurse was prepared to give her the answers. Offer her the opportunity of 'hands-on' experience.

"Would you like to give Matthew his bottle, Mrs. Smyth?" she enquired.

"I would love to," Frances replied. "But you will have to keep me right."

"Easy enough," the nurse was so helpful. "All you have to do is wind him at the front. You cant touch his back, obviously."

Frances took the tiny morsel of humanity on her knee for the first time, and fed him.

She returned to the hospital day after day, when Donika was out at the Segal House Nursery School.

"We will have to show you how to change the dressing on his back, Mrs. Smyth," a sister told Frances one day.

The lesion was like a massive tumour. It was transparent. All the veins could be clearly detected inside. There was a spot where a layer of skin was missing and it leaked. So it had to be dressed.

Frances soon learnt how to do the dressing. And took responsibility for it when she visited the hospital.

A consultant spoke to her about little Matthew.

"If your husband and you are willing to take this child on, and give him a home," he assured her, "you will have this hospital right behind you. Just ask at any time if you need any thing."

So they took him on. Brought him home.

And everybody took to him instantly.

They all loved him. He was so utterly loveable.

Though he had spina bifida, he was especially bright. There was an alert twinkle in his infant eyes.

And he was to be in and out of hospital so often.

The first time was in June. When he was just over two months old.

He had to have a shunt inserted into the left side of his head, for hydrocephalus. And he needed to have a hernia operation, as well.

This took the most of the month.

Then he came home again. Although the others loved him, they didn't like to see their mother changing the dressings on Matthew's back.

It was too distressing for them.

The boys, especially, kept well out of the way at first. Even Eric, who doted on little Matthew often found an excuse to get offside, if at all possible.

Frances accommodated them when she could by changing the dressings when no-one else was around.

Karen became a great help. After an initial coming-to-terms with Matthew's condition she learnt to do the dressings, too.

Matthew seemed to be progressing satisfactorily.

Everything seemed to be going well.

Then, in the late summer of 1992, when he was fifteen months old, the thing which nobody wanted to happen began to happen.

The lesion on his back started to break down. Leak in more places. This called for immediate action.

Major surgery.

Matthew was admitted to hospital on 28th September, 1992 and had a major operation the next day.

It was tricky, very skilled surgery, which lasted for six hours.

To have his back closed.

What a tense day that was! The surgeons had only given Matthew a fifty-fifty chance of survival.

It was all or nothing stuff.

This was the crunch.

Much fervent prayer was made for him.

Family, friends and the folks from the Jesus Saves Mission all cried to God.

And Matthew pulled through.

Much to everyone's delight and thanks to the power of prayer and the skill of the surgeons.

In September 1993 Matthew started school, in Fleming Fulton Nursery School.

He proved to be a bright and popular pupil.

Learning to zoom about in his wheelchair!

# CHAPTER TWENTY-SIX

# BRIGHT DAYS, BLACK DAYS

---

1993 WAS ELECTION YEAR AGAIN, AND ERIC BELIEVED THAT HE WAS NOW IN THE PLACE WHERE GOD WANTED HIM TO BE.

And stood for re-election.

In the pre-election campaigning Eric did as he had done on the two previous occasions.

Walked around the ward. Talked to the people.

He also spoke to them about his Christian faith and the happiness and satisfaction which it had brought to him.

It gave him untold pleasure, in the course of his visitations, to meet a lady in her eighties in Sugarfield Street. This elderly woman was concerned about life. And death. And the beyond.

Eric was able to spend some time with her, eventually leading her to faith in Christ.

Election day was Wednesday, 19th May.

Next morning, Eric had an appointment at the Royal Victoria Hospital. He sat there, waiting, for ages. It seemed like hours.

All the time his mind was turning to the count at the City Hall.

How would it go this time?

When, finally, he was free to go, Eric drove down the Grosvenor Road. He was making post-haste for the count.

In the course of a round-up of election analysis and predictions the voice from the car radio stated, in a matter-of-fact tone, "Eric Smyth of the DUP is doing well in Court Ward."

"Praise the Lord!" Eric shouted.

After completion of the first count, Smyth, Eric, had polled 2383 votes.

He had topped the poll and was elected at the first count.

All the hard work for his local community and standing-up for his Christian principles had paid-off.

The electorate had shown their approval by more than doubling his previous vote, and God seemed to have stamped His seal of approval on Eric's witness for Him, as well.

Eric was happy.

But there was a dark day ahead.

Saturday 23rd October, 1993.

Andrew had just returned from having been shopping on the Shankill, and was explaining to Frances, his mum, what he had, and hadn't bought when ... BANG!

There was a tremendous hollow boom.

The house shook. The windows rattled.

The groceries danced about on the table.

Loose items clattered to the floor.

"That must have been a bomb!" Frances said to Eric's mum and dad, who had called to see them. "And it sounded very close."

It wasn't long before her assumption was proved correct.

Mark came dashing into the house, yelling, "Mummy, mummy, where are you? Are you all right? Where are Donika and Matthew?"

He had heard that there had been a bomb on "the Road" and that children had been hurt. Knowing that his mum always went shopping with the kids on a Saturday morning he couldn't wait to find out if they were safe.

Frances phoned Eric, who was attending a DUP Conference in Dungannon.

He was shocked. Stunned. Appalled.

When he had informed Dr. Paisley, a few more hasty telephone calls were made.

As the full horror of what had happened on the Shankill Road began to filter through, it was decided to abandon the conference.

Eric drove home at speed.

What confronted him, when he arrived back on his home patch, was a scene of utter desolation.

A fish shop had just disappeared from the street.

It was lying in a dusty heap of tangled bricks, beams, slates and glass. There was a great gaping hole to the sky where it had been.

Police, soldiers, and civilians were all clawing at the rubble with their bare hands.

Trying to save the lives of innocent people, who an hour beforehand had been chatting, shopping, going about their business.

There was an air of disbelief.

Some of the bystanders cried out in stricken rage.

Many just sobbed silently.

The plaintive wail of ambulance sirens hung on the autumn air.

Many people had been badly injured.

Nine had lost their lives.

A man, his wife and child had been wiped out.

Blown off the face of the earth.

Eric visited the homes of all the victims. He had known many of them. And their families.

Some of them were Christians.

As he toured the homes, trying to console grieving relatives, Eric encountered a mixture of emotions.

People were devastated. People were angry.

Everyone was asking, "Why?" "Why?"

"Why this waste?"

Counselling those grief-stricken relatives and badly injured victims through the dark and difficult days that followed, was one of the most painful tasks that Eric Smyth, councillor and minister, had ever undertaken.

He was touched by the hope of a relative of a decimated family, who said to him, through her tears, "Thank God they were ready. We will see them all again some day. In heaven."

What faith!

What hope!

What consolation!

# CHAPTER TWENTY-SEVEN

# HEARTBREAK

---

DURING THE UPS AND DOWNS OF THE DONIKA-AND-MAT-THEW DAYS, AND DURING THE TOTALLY DOWNS OF THE BOMB-ON-THE-SHANKILL DAYS, ERIC AND FRANCES HAD ANOTHER CONSTANT WORRY.

It was to do with two of their own boys. Mark and Keith.

Something was happening to them.

Something which their parents didn't understand, at first.

Both boys' natures began to change.

Mark and Keith used to be normal lads. Liked a bit of fun. Were pleasant at home. Respected their parents.

Now they had become unpleasant. Wearisome to work with.

Nasty even.

They began to shout and yell about the house, often using foul language. They kicked doors. They hammered on the furniture with their fists.

But the most difficult thing of all to take was the abuse.

The verbal abuse of their mother, who loved them so much.

One night Eric could stand it no longer. He took a bold but desperately painful decision.

He ordered them out.

Told them to go and find accommodation elsewhere, until they learnt to live as normal family members again. As once they had done.

The problem with the boys was drugs.

The use of them. The sale of them.

Mark was first to become involved. He had started up in business on his own, then found himself in financial difficulties.

Not wanting to lose face, yet not knowing where to find help he began to sell drugs. To make quick money.

But it didn't, it couldn't last.

One bleak winter's night in January 1994, the car which Mark was driving was stopped by a police patrol.

All the occupants were ordered out.

The car was searched. Mark and his passengers were searched.

Mark had drugs in his possession.

Drugs were also discovered in the car boot.

Mark was taken away "for questioning".

Later that day a despondent group of young people made their way round to the Smyth home. There were three of them. Keith and his girlfriend, and Mark's girlfriend-of-the-moment. Keith was the spokesman.

"We just thought we had better tell you, before anybody else does, that Mark has been lifted for drugs" was the simple but sickening message that they brought.

Eric and Frances were devastated.

Their hearts fell to their boots.

Their eyes filled up. And overflowed.

Their stomach's turned over.

Their legs became shaky and felt all funny. Oh no!

They didn't realise it then, on that night of terrible tidings that it was only going to be the first of many, many sleepless nights.

They were heading straight into a storm of trial. Their faith in God was to be tested to the utmost in the days ahead.

Next day Eric and Frances were informed that their son was being detained in Crumlin Road Prison.

Eric had been in there many times to visit the prisoners. Often at the request of heartbroken parents.

As he entered that prison that day, to find his own son, he knew how they felt.

He was now a heartbroken parent himself.

When he realised how deeply involved Mark had been in the drugs scene, and now Keith's nature, like Mark's had undergone such a profound change for the worse, Eric recognised that he ought to seek out Keith right away. And caution him. Warn him off.

This he did. Father challenged son. Warned him of the dangers of drugs. Pointed to the mess that Mark had made of himself.

Keith denied any involvement.

A second, almost killer punch was delivered to Eric and Frances, then, in February 1994, when Jonathan and Keith's girlfriend Louise came round to the house, late one night. They were pale and shaking.

"There has been a big police raid on Kelly's up in Portrush," they said, "Keith has been lifted now, too."

When they were just trying to come to terms with Mark's arrest now this!

What a double blow!

Now Eric hadn't just one son to visit in custody in Crumlin Road prison.

He had two!

How could he advise other people about their families when two of his own sons were in jail?

What annoyed him most, however, was not the fact that the boys were being kept in custody. It was that they didn't seem to consider for one minute the implications of what they had been involved in.

They didn't seem to care a hoot that they were selling drugs which could kill other young people. Wreck other lives. Destroy other families.

In this respect, he and Frances were both glad that they had been apprehended. Before they had killed somebody else's son or daughter. Spread the misery to another set of parents.

The two young men were both released in March, to await trial.

Mark was married to Elizabeth in the summer of 1994, and his trial took place in September, in Ballymena Courthouse.

The police testified that they had been surprised to see Mark. Up until his arrest he hadn't been known to them on the drugs scene.

Mark alleged that he had been framed. The fact of the matter remained though he had been caught with drugs on his person and in his car.

A serious offence.

Mark was found guilty, and sentenced to three  years imprisonment.

The other occupants of the car walked free.

Keith's trial was held a year later. Again in Ballymena Courthouse.

He was found guilty of drugs offences.

And sentenced to nine months imprisonment.

The two sons were both in the same prison. Again.

Magilligan this time.

Those were two nightmare years for the distraught parents.

They couldn't sleep at nights. Made cups of tea.

Sat up in bed and talked.

Sat down in the kitchen in the cold in the middle of the night, and talked.

All the time they were asking themselves secretly, and asking each other openly, the question of hundreds of heartsore parents the world over.

"Where did I go wrong?"

"Where did we go wrong?"

The boys had both been brought up in a Christian home. They had heard the Bible read at home and in Church. They had been prayed for since before they were born.

Why had they rebelled?

Despite the heart-rending personal hurt for Eric and his wife, there were always public appearances to be made.

Eric had to go to work in the City Hall.

Councillor Smyth.

He had to mount the pulpit in the Jesus Saves Mission Church every Sunday.

Rev. Smyth.

This was difficult. Formidable, almost.

Some people wondered that "young people brought up in a Christian home," would become involved in the drugs scene.

"Stoop down so low," was an unkind term that was used.

When given the opportunity Eric explained to these people that Christianity, as the Bible taught it, was a personal matter. Being brought up in a Christian home didn't make his sons Christians.

Christians were people who had made an individual and personal commitment to Christ.

Some of the most cutting comments were made by members of the paramilitary groups who stood around at the street corners. When Eric stopped the minibus at various points to pick up or leave off children for the Jesus Saves Mission they would call, "Oh look! There's Eric Smyth! The REVEREND Eric Smyth. He's a minister, you know! But his sons are drug dealers. They are inside  at the minute. Doing time. Magilligan, Eric, isn't it?"

It was hard to stick.

Very, very hard to stick.

The media were sympathetic mostly.

Newspapers and television covered the stories.

Eric never dreamt that the God who was leading him into public life was also going to lead him into, and through, some of the most turbulent and testing days of his family life.

In the full glare of publicity.

In the full focus of the dreaded Public Eye (the Public has only one eye. Eric reckons it is enough).

During sleepless nights and depressing days two things proved to be a tremendous source of comfort to Eric and his wife.

The first was the support of so many people, from all sections of the community, and from many shades of political opinion, and religious persuasion.

They admired the sheer honesty and candour of Eric as he unreservedly denounced drug-taking and drug-dealing. Condemning openly what his sons had done, whilst never ceasing to love them as a father.

The heartsick parents greatly appreciated the concern of so many genuine people who sent cards and letters and made comforting phonecalls.

Yet there was always this churning inside of them. A sense of smarting and suffering seemed to grow and gurgle deep in their very innermost being, where kind words, whether spoken or written, never seemed to reach.

They found that the only panacea for this pain was prayer. Talking to God. For long periods, sometimes hours, at a time.

God who had brought them into the trial would bring them through, and out on the other side, they knew.

They just had to keep talking to Him. And they did.

So did others, too.

The elders, deacons and congregation of the Jesus Saves Mission were a continual tower of strength. They prayed, and prayed and prayed.

Mark and Keith have now completed their prison terms and have been released.

They have finished with drugs, and have both secured permanent employment.

That nightmare would seem to be over.

Yet, Eric and Frances have another, lasting concern for these two sons. Like they have for all of the family.

They would love to see them all united in faith in Christ. See the circle unbroken.

Eric often seeks comfort and assurance from the words of Peter, speaking on the day of Pentecost, when he said,

"Repent, and be baptised every one of you in the name of Jesus Christ for the remission of sins, and ye shall receive the Holy Ghost

For the promise is unto you, and to YOUR CHILDREN ..." Acts 2:38-39

The God who has promised, will deliver

No doubt about that.

Eric knows. And Frances knows.

They have proved it before.

But the waiting is sometimes tough ...

# CHAPTER TWENTY-EIGHT

# FIRST CITIZEN SMYTH

---

WHEN REV. ERIC SMYTH WAS PROPOSED FOR THE OFFICE
OF LORD MAYOR OF BELFAST, THE SUGGESTION MET WITH
RIDICULE FROM SOME OF HIS FELLOW COUNCILLORS.

Outright opposition from others.

"Sure he is a DUP man. He would be no good as Lord Mayor, for
he wouldn't meet the Roman Catholic community," some critics claimed.

Others cast doubt on the ability of a man who was dyslexic, and
still had trouble with the reading of unfamiliar texts, to hold such an
important office.

The Unionist parties in he City Hall pledged Eric their support.
That was encouraging, but not good enough on its own, for him. He
needed something more.

He needed the approval of his Heavenly Guide.

He needed assurance. And it came.

One evening in early May, 1995 Eric was reading his Bible at
home. It had been a busy day, full of bustle and bluster and talk of the
election of the new Lord Mayor.

As he read, that evening, in his own way and for his own comprehension, he came upon words which he had read so often before. Words which had meant much to him on many occasions. Yet they seemed to appear clothed in the freshness of spring, as he studied them.

They were in the tenth verse of Psalm forty-six.

"Be still, and know that I am God."

What good advice!

Eric had been scuttling about all day, talking to various councillor friends.

To "be still" would be hard! But he would have to try! Throughout the month of May, many laughed at the prospect of a semi-literate, "good-living" DUP Lord Mayor.

"You must be joking!" they chortled. "Eric Smyth is a nice enough man, I suppose. But he will never get enough support when it comes to the vote."

When Eric felt the sting of their jibes, he remembered his verse. "Be still, and know," it said.

He would know. They would know. The entire city of Belfast would know.

Know what?

Know that Eric Smyth had an all-powerful God acting as pilot at the helm of his life.

When election night came God demonstrated that power. The Unionist parties kept their promises and gave him their votes.

And Eric Smyth was elected Lord Mayor of Belfast.

The knew Lord Mayor, the Lord Mayor whom some believed would never make it, thanked those who had loyally supported him, and praised the God of his life who had made the "impossible" happen.

Now they would know that He was God indeed.

To demonstrate his desire to serve all sections of the community in his city, Eric Smyth has an SDLP deputy, Alasdair McDonald.

Many said it would never work.

They have been proved wrong.

It has.

Many said that Rev. Eric Smyth, a fundamentalist DUP councillor, wouldn't be accepted by a high percentage of the citizens of Belfast.

They have been proved wrong on that one, too.

He has been accepted, and is indeed respected, by the majority of the decent, hard-working, people of the city.

When elected to the position of Lord Mayor, it was hardly surprising that Eric Smyth chose Spina Bifida as the theme charity for his year in office. He pledged himself to raising money to help parents who couldn't afford the special, and very expensive, wheelchairs for their severely handicapped children.

This venture has proved both popular and successful.

A committee has been set up to operate this charity and its members have worked extremely hard.

Eric's sheer enthusiasm for the cause has inspired them, and the appearance of the magnetic Matthew on a number of public occasions has brought home to people the sheer extent of the disability.

In addition to fund-raising for his chosen charity, Eric has been a leader on another front.

In the campaign against drug abuse.

As one who lived through the trauma of seeing two sons serving prison sentences for drugs offences, he knows what he is talking about. And it shows.

Shortly after his election to Lord Mayor, Eric Smyth was introduced to Grainne Kenny, Chairwomen of EURAD - Europe Against Drugs. He was impressed by the tireless fervour of this campaigner, and was pleased to accept her invitation to represent Belfast at a conference of European Cities Against Drugs.

Through his involvement with anti-drugs crusading Eric has had a number of contacts with the Lord Mayor of Dublin, Councillor Sean Dublin Bay-Rockall Loftus.

These two Lord Mayors were interested to discover on meeting, that they both have a common interest in Spina Bifida!

So those who laughed and jeered, smirked and sneered, have been proved wrong.

Those who predicted that it wouldn't, it just couldn't work, have been proved wrong.

Why?

Complicated legal documents, and involved minutes of meetings, can prove very difficult for Eric. True enough.

The constant round of meetings, consultations, functions and representations can prove very tiring for Eric. True enough.

But the Lord Mayor of Belfast, Councillor Rev. Eric Smyth has a number of factors surrounding him which have contributed to his obvi- ous enjoyment of his position as First Citizen.

He has a tremendous capacity for work.

He has a genuine interest in people.

He is encouraged by an understanding and supportive Lady Mayor- ess.

He is helped and advised by wise and experienced party mem- bers.

He is surrounded by a friendly and diligent staff.

But above and beyond all the mortal aides that he may have, Eric Smyth has introduced into the Lord Mayor's suite at the City Hall a sense of the Immortal.

The man, who was once criticised for having a New Testament open on his machine in the Michelin factory is now respected for having his Bible open on the Lord Mayor's desk.

There is a real sense of the presence of God in there.

Often, before an important function, Eric bows in prayer and com- mits himself into Heavenly Hands.

"Lord, help me today," he sometimes prays. Very simply, very sincerely.

Or his prayer is often more specific.

"Lord, please help me through this one. Guide me as to what I should say."

And his prayer is always answered.

Those who hear him speak are impressed by his unscripted Chris- tian sincerity.

He has been still in the presence of the Almighty.

And KNOWS that He is God.

# CHAPTER TWENTY-NINE

# THE PRESIDENT, AND THE PRINCE OF PEACE

---

THE CHIEF EXECUTIVE OF BELFAST CITY COUNCIL SPOKE TO ERIC ONE DAY. HE SEEMED UNUSUALLY, ALMOST UNBELIEVABLY PLEASED.

"There is a possibility that the President of the United States, Bill Clinton, will be visiting us here in Belfast, later on in the year, Eric," he announced.

"When?" was Eric's first query.

"Depends a lot on the progress of the peace process, I suppose," the Chief Executive replied.

"Could he switch on the Christmas tree lights outside the City Hall?" the Lord Mayor suggested. "That would be a great chance to bring everybody together."

"Yes, he possibly could, if the date was right," came the thoughtful response. "But then what about the Power Rangers?"

The Power Rangers, many children's favourites, had been booked to come.

They sat thoughtfully for a few minutes.

The Power Rangers or A Very Powerful Man?

"Let's have them both, if possible," was the conclusion that they came to. The more the merrier, to promote a brighter, peaceful Belfast.

The Power Rangers were the first to come, on Thursday 16th November. They entertained more than one thousand children in the City Hall. They travelled out to a number of Special Care Schools.

The Power Rangers visit had been a resounding success.

Now the way was open for the President.

First to come were the great man's aides and advisers.

The place swarmed with them. Talking about security, arranging functions, discussing guest lists ...

The Mayor of Nashville sent a Christmas tree.

The American Consul attended to watch its erection in the City Hall grounds.

Yet more advisers, planners and security personnel arrived.

The excitement was growing by the hour.

A group of programme planers made an appointment to see the Lord Mayor. They wanted to discuss his role in relation to the President's visit.

They had it all cut-and-dried.

Or so they thought!

"Lord Mayor, we would like you to share the platform with the President at the switching on of the Christmas tree lights. We want you to introduce the President. You will have one minute to speak."

One minute to speak!

That would never be enough!

"Hold on there," Eric replied, firmly but courteously, "I would need more than one minute to speak. I am the Lord Mayor here, you understand. This is my city. I want to give the President a really good welcome. And I couldn't do that in one minute. I won't take too long, don't worry, but please don't tie me down to a minute!"

Eric believed that this was one of the reasons why his God had placed him in the Lord Mayor's office in this particular year. He was going to be afforded the opportunity to speak to a worldwide audience, with the chance of not only introducing President Clinton, whom it was hoped would play a key role in he peace process in Northern Ireland, but also of introducing his Lord and Saviour Jesus Christ, who played a key role in the most comprehensive peace process every known to mankind.

He wasn't going to miss this once-in-a-lifetime challenge.

Thus it was agreed.

When the long-awaited day came, Thursday 30th November, 1995, Rev. Eric Smyth, as Lord Mayor was first to formally welcome President Clinton to the city of Belfast. This meeting took place at Mackies Engineering works on the Peace Line.

Eric was impressed with the President from their very first encounter. Bill Clinton had obviously 'done his homework'. He seemed to know a surprising amount about Eric Smyth and his family, about Mackies, about Belfast, about peace ...

And it seemed that nobody had even had a chance to tell him anything yet!

Throughout the afternoon, when the President and First Lady were fulfilling a number of engagements throughout the Province, the Lord Mayor remained in  he City Hall.

He was very, very nervous.

As the time for the switching on of the Christmas tree lights approached, Eric fell on his knees in the Lord Mayor's parlour.

"Lord, please help me tonight," he prayed, fervently, possibly for the hundredth time.

"Just give me the wisdom to know what to say and do, and give me the strength and courage to do it."

There was a knock at the door.

It was Ann, the Lord Mayor's attendant.

"Lord Mayor, it is time for you to go out and meet the President," she said simply.

Eric was ready. Dressed in the full regalia of his office, and clutching his Bible, he set out.

Dozens of dignitaries and important American visitors had gathered in a large room waiting for the Lord Mayor to lead them down into the courtyard to welcome the President.

Eric's voice rose above the hushed nervous whispering and shuffling.

"I would like us to pray together," he said.

There followed a reverent silence when Rev. Eric Smyth commended the proceedings of the evening into the hands of his God, praying a blessing upon the President and First Lady, all who would take part in the ceremony, the thousands of people waiting outside and the worldwide television audience.

Then they all filed slowly, nervously, down the marble staircase.

When President Clinton and his wife stepped out of their limousine in the City Hall courtyard, the first thing that struck Eric and his waiting friends as remarkable was how fresh they both looked. After a hectic day's engagements they both appeared so spry and sprightly.

It almost seemed as though the City Hall was their first stop of the day!

Eric welcomed the Presidential pair for the second time. Not to Belfast this time, but to its City Hall.

As they walked through to the front of the building, the President chatted away. He told Eric that they had been touched by the spontaneous enthusiasm of the welcome that they had received in the Province.

He remarked upon the very attractively decorated Christmas tree in the foyer of the City Hall.

And it was nothing to the one that was waiting outside.

As they mounted the platform at the front of the City Hall, and looked down all that could be seen in any direction were upturned faces. Thousands of people, some estimates put the figure at one hundred thousand, gazed up at them.

Eager. Excited. Expectant.

The Lord Mayor welcomed the President of the United States and his wife, Hillary, to Belfast, yet again.

He spoke of the Christmas season. A time for children. A time for families.

Then he took the opportunity, which he genuinely believed that his God had afforded to him, to mention the true meaning of Christmas.

What it was all about.

How it all started.

The reason for the season.

He told of the coming into the world of the Lord Jesus Christ, the Christ of Christmas, as a baby in Bethlehem. The One who had come to bring peace on earth.

A Man of Peace. The Prince of Peace.

Then, opening his Bible which he still carried, Eric read these words from Matthew chapter one:

*"And she shall bring forth a son, and thou shalt call his name Jesus: for he shall save his people from their sins ...*

*Behold, a virgin shall be with child, and shall bring forth a son, and they shall call his name Emmanuel, which being interpreted is, God with us ..."*

Some people in the crowd booed.

"We want Clinton. We want Clinton ..." the chant began, drowning out the words of Scripture.

Clinton they wanted.

And it was Clintons they got. Both of them.

Hillary Clinton, the First Lady of the United States of America spoke first. In the course of her speech she thanked the Lord Mayor and the people of Belfast and Northern Ireland for their welcome and referred warmly to what the First Citizen had said.

Then the President spoke.

Everyone was enthralled.

The President of the United States on a platform in Belfast!

It seemed incredible!

He also alluded to the Lord Mayor's message and thanked the people for the tremendous welcome they had been given in the Province.

Then came the moment. The big switch on ...

The Christmas tree sprang ablaze with white lights that cut into the blackness of the November night.

The crowds were happy when they had heard the President, seen the lights and watched the fireworks.

The President and his wife were happy. And took great pains to say so, repeatedly. One of the most memorable days in their lives was how they described it.

Rev. Eric Smyth, Lord Mayor of Belfast, was deeply content, too despite the booing.

He had told a worldwide audience about his Saviour, whom he loved, and why He had come into the world.

And what was more, the President seemed to approve of his action.

When his wife was speaking, President Clinton had leaned across the platform, touched Eric on the knee and said, "Thank you, Lord Mayor, for reading the Word of God".

Those ten words, from the most powerful man on earth, were an encouraging endorsement.

An added bonus.

# CHAPTER THIRTY

# 'THE COMMON PEOPLE HEARD HIM GLADLY'

---

JUST AFTER CHRISTMAS, 1995, ERIC WAS OUT SHOPPING ON THE SHANKILL ROAD WITH HIS WIFE, FRANCES. THEY HAD DONIKA AND MATTHEW WITH THEM.

As they were just about to enter a shop, Eric was aware of a voice calling him. "Lord Mayor, Lord Mayor," it said.

Stopping in his step, Eric turned to see an elderly man approaching him. "Lord Mayor, I have been looking for you on 'the Road' to tell you how great it was, the way you spoke, you know, with President Clinton, yon night."

The little man was breathless, but sincere.

"Did you think so?" Eric asked, not knowing quite how to respond.

"Aye, I did indeed," his friend went on. "The way you read the Bible and spoke about the meaning of Christmas, and all. It was really good, and I wanted to tell you that."

Having said his bit, and without further ado, he hurried off down the footpath.

That has been Eric's experience so many times since that memorable last night in November, 1995.

He was out at a function in the Culloden Hotel, hosted by Paul Clarke of UTV. There were many celebrities attending. A successful businessman came across to Eric at the interval and said, "Lord Mayor, you don't know me. I'm a different faith from you. But I would just like you to know that I admire the stand that you took at the switching on of the Christmas tree lights."

A woman from Ballymurphy phoned into the City Hall.

"I would like to speak to the Lord Mayor," she requested.

When the Lord Mayor took the call, she had something of the same sort of message to convey.

"I'm a nationalist, Lord Mayor, and I don't agree with your politics. But I would just like to thank you for the way you spoke at the Christmas tree."

Letters, cards and telephone calls of support and approval have been received in the City Hall from all parts of the British Isles.

One of the most touching messages came from a man who had been sick. He said, "I was lying in my bed that day, watching television. I was so weak and sick that I couldn't get up. When you read that verse, Lord Mayor, it brought home to my heart the real reason why Jesus came. He shall save His people from their sins."

Perhaps the most heart-warming message of his year in office, came not from the President's visit, but as a direct result of his public and open condemnation of his sons' drug-dealing activities.

A woman from Sandy Row phoned Eric one day in the late autumn of 1995.

"I would like to tell you, Lord Mayor, about what has happened to me," she began, "I saw you on the TV a few nights ago, bravely condemning what your sons had done. You know, that touched a hidden chord in my heart ..."

Then she proceeded to explain.

"Your wife's grandmother used to speak to us when we were children. She used to tell us that she was praying for us. Praying that we would get saved ...

When I saw you on the television I remembered you and Frances, and the old lady who cared so much for us. It all came back to me, everything that I had heard, and I just simply trusted Christ as my Saviour."

As he stands looking out of the window of his office in the City Hall, watching the people and traffic hurrying to and fro in Donegall Square; the Lord Mayor, Rev. Eric Smyth, occasionally allows his mind to meander back down the years.

The lad from the humble home who has met the President of the United States ...

The heartbroken parent who has campaigned tirelessly to avoid heartbreak for hundreds of other parents ...

The young man who thought that he was rich when his wage was increased to ten guineas, but has now raised thousands of pounds for Spina Bifida ...

The Mission Hall minister who has spoken to millions on global TV ...

He remembers his school teacher.

"Smyth, you will never make anything of yourself," is what he had said.

And the man had been right.

'Smyth' could never have made anything of himself.

But God could take him, mould him and make him.

Make something of him.

And He did.